Feel Good Food

Feel Good Food

Wholefood recipes
for happy, healthy living

tony chiodo

hardie grant books
MELBOURNE · LONDON

Contents

A journey through food

My journey through cooking and food has been an exciting and evolving one. In my enthusiasm to discover the flavours and qualities of different cuisines throughout the world, I have travelled widely and experienced a level of self-discovery that I had never expected.

It all began growing up in an Italian family where food was enjoyed as a festivity. Every year we made our own tomato sauce and sausages, with homemade wine fermenting away in the garage every autumn. Our compact garden was always bursting with produce – in summer, corn, rocket (arugula) and zucchini (courgette) flowers thrived, while silverbeet (Swiss chard), broad (fava) beans and pumpkin dominated the winter vegie patch. At the time, the idea of eating out was unthinkable. I took for granted the now fashionable notion of eating locally grown, seasonal produce. Nothing was wasted and every meal was shared at a table, with family and friends – and always with a tablecloth and napkins.

I never set out to become a chef – I had my eye set on becoming a hotel manager. I just thought that training to become a chef would be a great step in that direction. To get my dreams underway, I became an apprentice to the *avant-garde* chef Jacques Reymond at Mietta's in Melbourne. This was during the height of *nouvelle cuisine* – precise French cooking with complex flavours and art-on-a-plate presentation. I was working in the midst of a food revolution, where experimentation with flavours and ingredients was at its peak. It was a long way from my mum's rustic home cooking – it was fashionable, exciting and I was hooked. I left my hotel management aspirations behind and went to work in the kitchen of Stephanie Alexander's eponymous Melbourne restaurant, where I was to master fine French cooking techniques with precision and finesse.

I was hungry for more culinary knowledge, so I pursued my Mediterranean heritage and accepted a scholarship at La Guida Italiana di Cucina, the Italian institute of traditional cuisine in Northern Italy. Here I discovered authentic Italian cooking – unlike anything I had seen back home. I cooked with wild game and greens, truffles and rare local mushrooms. I learnt how to make butter and creamy goat's cheese, wine, wood-fired bread and sausages at the laid-back restaurants in the countryside of Piemonte, Lombardia and Emilia Romagna. The cooking was earthy and real, yet still refined and complex in flavour. I was shown a deep respect for ingredients and how to add a part of yourself to the food. I thrived as I worked in other kitchens, from Franco Colombani's Albergo del Sole to the extravagant Michelin-starred Ristorante Gualtiero Marchesi.

I returned to Melbourne sated – but with myriad health concerns too painful to ignore. Despite the sensational dishes I'd been cooking and enjoying in my newfound career, I felt that certain foods had played a part in the demise of my health. I became fascinated by the relationship between food and health and felt drawn to discover the clean and simple flavours of Japanese cuisine. I travelled to Japan and was introduced to Zen meditation, shiatsu and aikido. The food I experienced there was balanced, with ingredients chosen for their healing qualities as much as their flavour. Eating became an art and a science. Healing food was having a beneficial effect on my ever thankful body.

After Japan, I travelled to India and began cooking in an ashram. This experience strengthened my belief that food could promote health and awakened me to its effect on enhancing the spirit. I developed patience with my cooking. I also discovered the importance of the right attitude when preparing food – a lesson sharply learnt when I was ordered out of the kitchen for being too angry. Food prepared with a happy, loving heart will nourish, while food prepared with an angry attitude may leave the recipient with indigestion, no matter how fine the ingredients. I began to develop an intuitive cooking sense, as I slowly accepted that cooking and eating are nourishing activities, central to our sense of well-being.

Balanced and grounded, I returned to Australia to bring all these influences together. Wild Rice Wholefoods Café was my first stop, and it became a fertile playground for exploration and creativity. Here I was free to cook with abandon, using organic and biodynamic ingredients. I then embarked on my own venture with Café Angelica, where I showcased my own personality and style of cooking. Feeding people fresh, vibrant wholefood was a joy and motivated me to discover the benefits and qualities of these seemingly magical foods in more depth.

Thirsty for more, I moved to America to study at the Kushi Institute in Boston. It was here that I learnt about the *yin* and *yang* of food: how to combine flavours, textures and ingredients to bring an unbalanced body back to life. I discovered ingredients such as kuzu, daikon and umeboshi, and as I learnt about and ate these potent foods, I felt my own body becoming stronger and more resilient. I graduated as a macrobiotic and wholefoods teacher, signalling the beginning of a passionate love affair with wholefood cooking.

Many years later, I returned home to Melbourne and founded the Grainaissance Wholefoods Cooking School. My aim was to inspire others to include my unique blend of wholefoods in their daily lives. While teaching, I discovered that people yearned for simple, healthy food, which was flavoursome and full of character. So, I began to combine more of the traditional flavours and dishes of the Mediterranean with the health-supportive foods and principles of Asian cookery. The result of this combination is fresh and clean food that is easy to prepare and brings satisfaction to both the body and mind.

This pairing of Mediterranean and Asian cuisines, with an emphasis on wholefoods, forms the heart of all the recipes in *Feel Good Food*. All the ingredients have been carefully considered, in order to create a healthy, well-balanced dish that bursts with exciting flavour and sensory satisfaction. It's good food that can be integrated into everyday life. This book is for those people who wish to cook real food that will support health and life in a pure and natural way. Nothing could be simpler.

The thought of cooking with new and unusual foods can seem a little daunting at first, but trust me, it won't take long before you get the hang of it. You can approach this book any way you wish – there are no step-by-step instructions and no right or wrong. Simply throw yourself into the cooking and take your own journey.

The most important advice when venturing into the world of wholefoods, is to accept that there may be a few failures and re-inventions on the journey – such as when my light and fluffy grain pilaf turned into a soggy mess before I managed to turn it into a palatable meal. It's only through mistakes that new horizons can be met, and it's through this ongoing process of trial and error that you'll come to develop your own style of cooking.

But before you venture on, following are some tips that I've learnt on my own journey with wholefood cooking to help you along your way.

Buon appetito!
Tony Chiodo

Getting started

The wholefoods diet

Wholefoods are classified as foods that are as close to their natural state as possible. By consuming wholefoods, we obtain the vital nutrients not found in refined foods. Some wholefoods, such as nuts or seeds, can be eaten raw. Others, such as grains or legumes, need to be cooked before they're consumed. A modern wholefoods diet is also focused on including organic and biodynamic produce where possible.

Choosing organic and biodynamic

With organic and biodynamic foods becoming more mainstream, the question that invariably gets asked is – does buying and preparing these food matter?

Regular, non-organic foods are grown with a veritable chemical cocktail in order to produce the fast-growing, perfect-looking produce with a long shelf life found in most supermarkets. Certified organic food, by contrast, is free of pesticides, fungicides and fertilisers. Organic foods are also free from genetic modification – a practice of manipulating nature that may well prove to have far-reaching consequences for us all. Organic farming is a way of producing food without chemicals – just as nature intended.

Biodynamic farming is an enhanced form of organic farming, focused on activating the nutrients in soil, which in turn nurture and produce nutrient-dense crops. Biodynamic farming produces food with superior quality, flavour and nutritional value – nothing like the chemical-laden produce stocked in supermarkets.

From my experience, if the only change you made to your diet were to exclusively choose organic and biodynamic produce, your health would improve. Your body would no longer have to deal with all the added chemicals in your diet and you'd be enjoying foods with a superior flavour.

For those who would like to give this organic life a try, I'd recommend starting by switching to organic or biodynamic meat and dairy products. The hormones, antibiotics and other chemicals used to create fast-growing, milk- and meat-producing animals are not meant for human consumption. These chemicals create a burden on our digestive systems, which can lead to all sorts of allergies and other more serious health challenges.

The next foods to convert to organic or biodynamic should be fresh fruit, which taste just like they used to, before intensive farming took over. If you're convinced and want to go further, begin to buy your vegetables organically or biodynamically. Start with root vegetables, which take longer to grow so suck-up more chemicals from the soil when conventionally grown, followed by greens, such as broccoli, green beans and peas, and lastly, replace the leafy greens in your diet with organic or biodynamic varieties.

Of course, down the track, I would also recommend that all your grains, beans and other dried goods move into the organic or biodynamic realms. Your body will thank you.

The vegetarian diet

I'm often asked about vegetarian diets, as many of my dishes, including those in *Feel Good Food*, are meat-free. Although many people assume that if you follow a vegetarian diet you will miss out on vital nutrients, this is not the case. With some careful planning, and an understanding of what your body needs, you can follow a meat-free diet – or a diet with little meat – with no adverse effect to your health. This is what I do myself, and is what *Feel Good Food* promotes.

Most of us assume that calcium, which promotes healthy bones and great teeth, can only be sourced from meat and dairy. However, some of the best sources of calcium are found in the garden, especially from dark leafy greens, including kale, watercress and dandelion greens. Chinese cabbage, mustard greens, bok choy, broccoli and parsley are also good sources.

Away from the garden, seaweed not only provides good-quality iodine, but is one of the richest plant sources of calcium. Tofu (beancurd) that is produced using calcium sulphate (gypsum) or magnesium chloride (nigari) results in a calcium-rich food – so look for those ingredients on the label. Calcium can also be found in beans, nuts and seeds. Sesame seeds, which contain high levels of calcium, can be included in your diet by adding tahini (sesame seed paste) or by sprinkling fresh or toasted seeds over your food.

Iron is another nutrient that many people assume can only be obtained through animal sources. However it is possible to get enough iron through a vegetarian diet. Iron's major role in the body is in the formation of healthy red blood cells, which are essential for transporting oxygen around the body. Many of the calcium-rich foods mentioned above also contain good levels of iron. Seeds such as sesame and pumpkin are particularly good, as are cashews and almonds. The sea vegetables wakame and kombu are also abundant in this blood-strengthening mineral. Wholegrains and beans, including soy bean products such as tofu and tempeh, are also good iron sources. Including vitamin C-rich foods in your diet, such as kiwi fruit and citrus, will help in the absorption of iron from plant foods.

One problematic nutrient for some vegetarians and vegans is vitamin B12, which is naturally found in meat and animal products. However, vegetarians who regularly consume eggs and milk products can obtain adequate supplies of this vitamin. There are also vegan sources of vitamin B12–fortified foods, such as cereals and soy products (including tempeh), unpasteurised miso and sea vegetables, such as wakame and kombu.

Not to be forgotten in a meat-free or meat-reduced diet is protein. The different amino acids that make up proteins are important for growth and tissue repair – they are the building blocks of the body. The best sources of vegetarian protein include beans, lentils, grains, nuts, seeds, tofu, tempeh, soy milk, yoghurt and free-range eggs.

Meat contains a complete range of amino acids which delivers a high level of protein to the body. As no plant food, other than quinoa, has a complete amino acid profile, it's a good idea to combine a range of vegetarian protein sources to provide the body with the full complement of amino acids. So, for example, eat tempeh with millet, baked beans with polenta or lentils with rice – the aim is to eat a wide variety of these foods and the body will do the mixing and matching.

Seasonal cooking

To get the best nutrition, flavour and quality from your food, begin to eat foods that are in season and grown close to home. This may feel limiting, but it will guarantee perfectly ripe food with abundant flavour that hasn't had to cross borders or oceans to reach you. Cooking seasonally and locally allows you to explore different recipes and cooking styles to match the mood of the year.

Spring – This is the season of expansion and a time when tender leafy greens should be making a regular appearance on your plate. Try spring onions (scallions), sprouts, Chinese greens, lettuce and herbs such as parsley and basil, and begin to lighten meals with citrus flavourings. The cooking style should lean towards blanching, pan-frying or grilling (broiling) as these are fresh and light methods of cookery.

Summer – In the warmer months, introduce light, cooling foods and include more raw foods at every meal. The cooking style should be quick, such as stir-frying or sautéing, to keep foods as fresh and raw as possible. Eat snow peas (mangetout), corn, broccoli, cucumbers, berries and stone fruit. It's also a great time to add fresh mint and coriander into meals for their cooling effects.

Autumn – When the temperature drops, it's time to turn towards a more warming cuisine. Include autumn harvest foods such as pumpkin, carrots, cabbage, onions and garlic. Add warmth and spice by including mustard seeds, ginger, peppercorns and cinnamon. Cooking styles should start to include braising and slow simmering.

Winter – This is the time to turn to deeply warming, nourishing foods. Include more root vegetables, grain and bean dishes, as well as more meat, poultry and fish for their strengthening qualities. The method of cookery during this season should be stewing, pressure cooking and oven baking.

Creating balance in cooking

The Chinese have been using food to support health and well-being for thousands of years – they consider that every food has an effect on the body, which can bring it back into balance and health, or throw it out of balance and into poor health. This concept forms the basis of macrobiotics. Without getting too involved with the principles of this food philosophy, there are a few points that help illustrate the idea of balancing your cooking for flavour and health.

Central to macrobiotics is the concept of *yin* and *yang*. They are terms that represent the opposing qualities that exist in all living things. Simply put, everything has an opposite – think of hot and cold, dark and light, rest and activity. Too much of one element will send you out of balance

and have you craving the opposing quality. We need to experience both *yin* and *yang* in order to live in harmony within ourselves.

The same concept applies when it comes to food. Certain foods, for example, are cooling to the body, such as cucumber and tofu, while others are warming, such as ginger and mustard. Another opposite that applies to food is that of 'contractive' and 'expansive'. For example, when something sweet is placed on the tongue it tends to expand, while a pinch of salt tends to make it contract. Whatever is happening on the tongue will also happen in the body. Foods are also either acid or alkaline. Even cooking styles influence the *yin* or *yang* nature of food.

It can sound complicated, but most people prepare foods with these principles in mind already. For example, we often serve a cooling salad or condiment with a spicy dish, or slow cook a casserole in winter to increase the heat and intensity of the food, or we may add a pinch of salt to a sweet dessert. These factors give new meaning to the notion of a 'balanced diet', however the message is the same – to have a balanced mind and body we need to eat in a balanced way.

Every dish in this book has been created with these opposites in mind – so that you can easily create meals that will satisfy the taste buds while harmonising your body and mood at the same time.

Flavour, colour and texture

When looking to produce dishes with that extra-special something, you will also need to consider flavour, colour and texture.

Flavour – The five flavours of food are sour, bitter, sweet, pungent and salty. It's the combination of these flavours that adds depth, lifting meals out of a one-dimensional state.

Try to include at least three flavours in each meal and you will begin to make magic:

Sour: lemons, limes, pickles and vinegar

Bitter: sesame seeds, dandelion greens, rye grain and alfalfa

Sweet: onions, pumpkins, carrots, sweet potato and cabbage

Pungent: ginger, horseradish, pepper, garlic and mustard

Salty: miso, shoyu, sea vegetables and sea salt

Colour – A colourful meal is always welcoming. As with flavour, try to introduce at least three different colours in every meal. The five desirable colours are green, red, orange/yellow, white and black. Not only will your plate look great, but according to macrobiotic principles, the food will harmonise better when it's being digested. If you're wondering which foods fall into the black category, think of black beans, sea vegetables, black sesame seeds and shoyu or tamari.

Texture – For texture, think about using different cooking styles in each meal to alter the sensation in the mouth. Stir-fried vegetables, for example, create a totally different feel than mashed or baked vegetables. If you're stuck in a boiling or steaming rut, then try to excite the food and taste buds once again.

Other ways you can add texture to a meal include adding raw foods to cooked foods for contrast and nutritional value, combining hearty grains with slippery greens or a raw salad with some toasted seeds and a creamy sauce. By throwing all these factors into the mix, your meals will become more exciting.

A note on sautéing

Be aware that all oils break down and create toxic substances at high heat. Therefore, if you want to sauté and have your oil too, try this method: add two to three tablespoons of water to the pan with the onion and once simmering, add your oil. This will prevent the oil heating to an extreme temperature and stop it becoming toxic. Also, be sure to use a more refined olive oil for sautéing over high heats rather than extra virgin olive oil, which is purer and breaks down more easily. Extra virgin olive oils are best used at lower heats, in salads or for dousing over a finished soup or dish.

The wholefoods pantry

You'll need to stock up on some basic ingredients before embarking on this new culinary adventure. Wander into your pantry and check that you've got a few essentials to help with your everyday cooking. Take a moment to clear out any old and out-of-date ingredients, as spices, flours, nuts and seeds have a limited shelf life – some go rancid, some attract weevils and some simply lose their vitality. Then you'll be ready to go out and re-stock the pantry. You don't have to go wild buying everything, but rather, stock up on small amounts and buy the best-quality produce you can afford.

A pantry filled with food gives you a good feeling. My rule is always to buy small amounts of dried foods, such as grains, beans and pastas, and to buy them often. Remove items from their packaging and slip them into large glass jars. Label them, if you like, noting the use-by date, just in case your range starts to expand. Oils, vinegars and condiments should be purchased in small bottles and restocked regularly.

Organise your pantry so that it becomes as streamlined as a mechanics workshop – the pantry must work for you. It's here that you decide to make either a magic meal, or opt for a takeaway. When you rearrange your pantry and kitchen to suit your cooking style, it will support and inspire you to cook and eat well. You'll become a clever and untroubled cook every time. Here are some of my must-have staples that will help you get started.

Grains and noodles

Grains have become my daily bread. I usually start the day with either porridge or bircher muesli. During the day, I select grains depending on the season and my mood. I find the most grounding and levelling food is short-grain brown rice. Other days I might include hulled millet, polenta, quinoa, couscous and barley. Grains are versatile and a great standby food suited to any time of the day.

For me, noodles are the ultimate in fast comfort food. I lean towards the Japanese buckwheat (soba) noodles and add them to miso-style broths, or I include the chilled green tea variety in summer salads. My other favourite is the Chinese fresh, flat rice noodles, for a quick and easy stir-fry, or dunked in a clear sweet and sour soup.

Beans and lentils

Beans and lentils are cheap, versatile and flavoursome foods. I love them all, but my favourite standbys are red lentils for a creamy soup, chickpeas (garbanzo beans) for salads, black beans for my spicy refried beans and red adzuki beans for casseroles. I also always have a variety of good-quality canned organic beans to hand for emergencies.

Nuts and seeds

The two essential nuts in my pantry are walnuts and almonds. I soak almonds overnight to make almond milk to pour over cereal or use in a smoothie. I chop walnuts into my breakfast porridge and grain pilafs, roast them for salads or simply snack on them raw.

My three seeds of choice are pumpkin (pepitas), sunflower and sesame. I soak a little of each in my porridge the night before. I also dry-roast them individually then drizzle with soy sauce for a great salty condiment or snack. Beware – it won't last long!

I always have unhulled tahini, which is sesame seed paste, and hazelnut and almond butters in the pantry. I use the tahini to thicken or enrich soups and dips, while the hazelnut and almond butter is heavenly on toast.

Savoury seasonings

Three types of sea salt sit on my bench: I use a grey, slightly moist, unrefined sea salt for everyday meal preparation; a white unrefined sea salt to make pickles; and Celtic sea salt to sprinkle over salads.

Another high-performance salt flavouring is miso. I have two in the refrigerator at all times. I try to get my hands on unpasturised varieties, as they're more beneficial to the gut due to their prebiotic nature – they also taste better. I use white (shiro) miso to flavour my soups, spreads and dips, as it's sweet and less salty than other miso varieties. I also use barley (mugi) miso, which is salty, dark, and nutritious – and gives my soups and sauces great depth.

Shoyu is a Japanese soy sauce, which is traditionally fermented to taste, like fine, aged wine. I use it to season soups and stir-fries. Tamari, a soy sauce with the wheat removed, has a stronger, more direct, flavour than shoyu which I use to marinate tofu and tempeh.

Sea vegetables are the dark pieces that you'll often see swimming in my soups, casseroles and sometimes in my pickles and salads. Kombu, being quite hardy, loves a long cooking time, so is included in most of the grain and bean soups in *Feel Good Food*. Wakame, which is softer, is good in soups but is great as a pickle, condiment or marinated in a salad.

A splash of mirin, a Japanese rice wine, to a stir-fry, soup, sauce, or even a grain or bean salad, rounds it off nicely. Being slightly sweet, it takes away any harsh edges.

Vinegar adds excitement to a dish. My everyday vinegar is a naturally fermented brown rice variety, which is slightly sweet and easy on the taste buds. I also love champagne vinegar as a salad dressing, balsamic splashed over blanched greens and apple cider vinegar in warm water, as a great mouth gargle first thing in the morning.

I also stock vegetable bouillon powder or stock cubes, for those moments when you haven't the time to make a stock.

My spices live close to the stove. I have the traditional Indian crew – cumin and coriander seeds and powder, mustard, fennel and fenugreek seeds and ground turmeric. I also stock the warming spices that I use in drinks or for sweets, such as cinnamon, cloves, nutmeg and cardamom. I shouldn't forget saffron for risottos and fish soup and smoked paprika and dried chillies for all things Moroccan.

My staple oils are unrefined, cold-pressed extra virgin olive oils for drizzling and dressings, more refined olive oil for cooking and dark roasted sesame oil for stir-frying. I also use an organic unrefined coconut oil in my cooking and for cakes and sweet pastries. Coconut oil imparts a delicate flavour and an added richness to sweets.

I always have at least six organic free-range eggs sitting in my fridge for making meals in minutes, to use as a binder when making burgers or to help raise cakes. The eggs used in this book are around 60 g (2¼ oz) each.

My pantry will also have some unbleached white and wholemeal spelt flour, unbleached white wheat flour, coconut and buckwheat flours and fine cornmeal (polenta). I'll vary them according to the result I'm after. These flours end up in pancakes, muffins and cakes.

Sweet flavourings

The sweet shelf in my pantry is always overflowing – it contains sweeteners such as maple and brown rice syrup, barley malt and apple and pear juice concentrates. These end

17

up in cakes and puddings and impart their own distinct flavour.

I use both good-quality natural vanilla extract and whole vanilla pods. Vanilla extract is used when you need vanilla right away, while the pods are sliced in half and added to simmering soy creams or for poaching fruit.

I also have a supply of raw cacao powder and desiccated (dried, shredded) coconut in my pantry, which are perfect for making great cakes.

Dried dates, apricots and raisins add sweetness to desserts and can be puréed into a paste to use as a sweet icing (frosting) over cakes and muffins.

Finally, I always have soy milk and a can of coconut cream to hand. Soy milk is great in my espresso-style dandelion coffee, in cakes and on porridge, while the coconut cream is for my Thai-inspired curries and sometimes drizzled over breakfast grains.

ty. Ltd.

MERC
ET, ADEL
OE
E 2

TELE
23 4
23 4

AN GROWN

A note about the recipes

So, you have a recipe page open, you've bought the ingredients and are now ready to make magic. Take a deep breath, relax and leave your dramas behind.

Every ingredient has a part to play within each recipe. Some are used for their health-supportive qualities, others to balance the flavours and textures of a meal, and others are there for their visual beauty.

The recipes have been designed and arranged with a purpose. If followed they will work, but if embraced they will shine. Once you've mastered a recipe, you can begin to improve on it by adding your own unique twist.

19

Breakfasts

For some people, breakfast is often ignored, while others find that they can't 'rev up' without some morning fuel. Making breakfast a priority is a great idea as it sets you up well for the day ahead. The recipes in this section will help you to make 'breaking the fast' a ritual you can't live without – just like a morning hug! We need nourishing foods that are gentle on our stomach and kick start our system at the same time.

Breakfast cereals are usually laden with sugar and salt, but are quick to prepare and, as they are so highly processed, easy to gulp down. These out-of-the-box meals are often eaten on the run without much thought, and helped down with a strong coffee or sugar-enriched juice. Other popular breakfasts, such as bacon and eggs, are high in saturated fats and place a huge burden on the system. Breakfast sets the tone for the rest of the day, so try to choose the right foods for your well-being.

Choose a wholegrain porridge filled with complex carbohydrates or a slightly salty soup, to inject you with high-quality energy for the day's activities. These types of breakfast are easy to digest, often easy to make and soothing to the stomach.

Keep breakfasts simple and give it thought the night before. Try soaking grains overnight to reduce cooking time in the morning.

Have some apple or pear butter or other toppings on hand to help transform an ordinary morning experience into something delicious. Roasted nuts, soaked seeds or toasted granola also add that morning excitement when needed.

If you need any extra sweetening, go for natural sweeteners such as rice syrup or a fruit juice concentrate. Flavour your breakfasts with natural vanilla extract and warming spices such as ground cinnamon and cloves or fresh ginger.

For a more flavoursome and filling porridge, stir through a spoonful of tahini or macadamia butter.

Like any meal, take note of the season. Cooked fruit compotes, such as apple or pear, are easily digested in the winter, while fresh berries are a refreshing, fun topping in the warmer months.

Breakfast need never be the same. Following are some of my jump-out-of-bed eye openers.

Almond milk

Almond milk is a great milk alternative with a subtle, nutty flavour. Use it in porridge, drizzle it over breakfast cereals or use as a milk substitute in pancakes and cake batters.

1 cup whole almonds
2 cups filtered, boiling water

Place the almonds in a jar and pour the boiling water over the top. Allow to sit for 15 minutes, or soak overnight.

When ready, pour the almonds and water into a food processor or blender and process until smooth. Pass the liquid through a fine sieve and discard the skins. Almond milk can be refrigerated for up to 3 days.

Makes 2 cups

Multi-grain bircher with apple and raspberries

This is a breakfast for a hot summer morning. Prepare most of it the night before and finish it off in minutes the next day. For a tropical variation, try soaking with orange juice and adding mango instead of the raspberries. If you like, you can also substitute walnuts and almonds for the seeds. This is a great morning starter with lots of roughage to prime the day.

Combine the oats, barley, quinoa, rye, sunflower seeds, sesame seeds, linseeds, vanilla and cinnamon in a bowl. Pour over the apple juice, stir through to combine, then cover and leave to soak overnight in the refrigerator.

To serve, fold through the yoghurt and top with the apple slices and raspberries.

Serves 4

¼ cup rolled (porridge) oats

¼ cup rolled barley

¼ cup quinoa flakes

¼ cup rye flakes

1 tablespoon sunflower seeds

1 teaspoon sesame seeds

1 teaspoon linseeds

1 teaspoon natural vanilla extract

½ teaspoon ground cinnamon

1 cup apple juice

1 cup plain yoghurt

2 granny smith apples, cored and finely sliced

150 g (5½ oz) fresh raspberries

Easy morning soup

This morning savoury soup is the perfect breakfast for a hangover – or any morning when you're feeling a little under the weather and need something soothing to start the day. Simmer the soup with some ginger strips or add ginger juice to really wake you up and warm you. The tofu isn't essential, but it adds protein and calcium to the dish.

Bring 4 cups water to the boil in a saucepan, add the onion and simmer for 2 minutes. Add the carrot and simmer for a further minute before adding the tofu.

Mix the miso in a bowl with 3 tablespoons of the soup liquid until the miso dissolves. Pour this back into the soup, add the bok choy and simmer for 2 minutes. Take off the heat and allow to settle for a few minutes before serving.

Serves 4

¼ red (Spanish) onion, finely sliced

½ carrot, cut into fine matchsticks

100 g (3½ oz) firm tofu, cut into 2 cm (¾ in) cubes

1 tablespoon white miso

4 bok choy (pak choy) stems, chopped

Scrambled tofu with sweet vegetables

This is a delicious scramble that's light, colourful and full of flavour. Have it over some toasted sourdough bread or next to some steamed brown rice or millet. I often stir in a little extra olive oil at the end for that extra boost.

Heat half the oil in a frying pan over medium heat and sauté the onion and garlic with a pinch of sea salt for 3 minutes, or until softened. Add the turmeric and 1 teaspoon water. Add the carrot, capsicum and corn kernels and sauté for 3–5 minutes.

Add the crumbled tofu to the pan and stir thoroughly. Reduce the heat to low and add $1/3$ cup water, cover and allow the mixture to steam for 5 minutes. Add some extra sea salt and the freshly ground black pepper with the basil, olives and remaining oil, and serve piping hot.

Serves 4

2 tablespoons olive oil

½ red (Spanish) onion, finely diced

1 garlic clove, crushed

sea salt

½ teaspoon ground turmeric

½ carrot, diced

¼ red capsicum (pepper), diced

1 corn cob, kernels removed

500 g (1 lb 2 oz) firm tofu, crumbled

¼ teaspoon freshly ground black pepper

2 tablespoons finely sliced basil

8 pitted black olives, sliced

Crêpe rolls with pumpkin and almond butter

This recipe takes a little time, so make the batter and pumpkin butter the night before. These crêpes make a fun mid-morning Sunday brunch that children can get their hands into. Experiment with different fillings – try adding crumbled tofu to the vegetables or refried black beans with avocado and tofu sour cream.

To prepare the crêpe batter, whisk the buckwheat flour, spelt flour and salt together in a large bowl and make a well in the centre. In a separate bowl, beat the egg, soy milk and oil together and pour into the well, working the flour into the egg mixture while gradually adding 1½ cups water. Whisk the batter until smooth and refrigerate for 30 minutes.

To make the pumpkin and almond butter, purée all the ingredients in a food processor until smooth and set aside.

To prepare the filling, heat the oil in a frying pan over medium heat and sauté the leek and sea salt for 3 minutes. Add the carrot, capsicum and cabbage to the pan and sauté for 3 minutes, or until the vegetables soften. Transfer to a bowl, fold through the parsley and set aside.

In a crêpe pan or frying pan, heat 1 teaspoon oil over medium heat then ladle in enough batter to thinly coat the pan. Cook for 3–4 minutes, or until the top side sets and the underside is golden. Gently lift and flip to cook the other side for 2–3 minutes. Transfer to a plate and repeat with the remaining batter.

To assemble, lay out each crêpe, arrange 1 tablespoon of the vegetable filling over half the crêpe and two slices of avocado. Fold the crêpe in half, then into quarters.

Just before serving, gently warm the pumpkin and almond butter and serve with the crêpes. You can eat them immediately or wait for everyone to get out of bed and reheat in the oven for 3 minutes before serving.

Makes 12

CRÊPE BATTER

1 cup buckwheat flour

1 cup unbleached spelt flour

1 teaspoon salt

1 egg

1 cup soy milk

1 tablespoon extra virgin olive oil, plus extra for frying

PUMPKIN AND ALMOND BUTTER

300 g (10½ oz) pumpkin, peeled and steamed until tender

2 tablespoons almond paste

3 tablespoons orange juice

pinch of sea salt

FILLING

1 tablespoon extra virgin olive oil

1 leek, white part only, cut into fine matchsticks

pinch of sea salt

½ carrot, cut into fine matchsticks

¼ red capsicum (pepper), cut into fine strips

200 g (7 oz) cabbage, finely shredded

1 tablespoon roughly chopped flat-leaf (Italian) parsley

½ avocado, finely sliced

Tofu French toast with lemon walnut syrup

This is my simple version of the famed French toast. It's fried, sticky and saucy – perfect for a pick-me-up brunch. Cook it gently in a non-stick pan and eat 'à la minute' with lots of lemony syrup.

Put the tofu, cinnamon, vanilla, miso, rice syrup, sea salt, kuzu and turmeric in a food processor and process to a smooth purée, then transfer to a bowl. Dip a slice of bread into the tofu mixture to lightly coat both sides. Repeat with the remaining slices.

Heat the oil in a large non-stick frying pan over medium heat. Add the coated bread to the pan and fry for 1–2 minutes on each side, or until golden brown.

To make the lemon walnut syrup, bring the rice syrup to the boil in a small saucepan, add the lemon juice and simmer for 1 minute then add the walnuts, stir through and quickly pour over the French toast.

Serves 4

250 g (9 oz) medium to firm tofu
1 teaspoon ground cinnamon
1 teaspoon natural vanilla extract
1 teaspoon white miso
1 teaspoon rice syrup
pinch of sea salt
1 tablespoon kuzu or arrowroot
1 teaspoon ground turmeric
4 slices sourdough bread
2 tablespoons macadamia or vegetable oil

LEMON WALNUT SYRUP
½ cup rice syrup
2 tablespoons lemon juice
¼ cup chopped roasted walnuts

Sweet quinoa and coconut morning pudding

This is a deliciously creamy and sustaining morning pudding that will delight children as well as grown ups. Eat it at room temperature on a hot day or enjoy it chilled as a dessert. If you like, substitute almond or coconut milk for the orange juice, and a ripe mango instead of the bananas – and let yourself bask in the flavours of the tropics.

Bring the orange juice to the boil in a saucepan over medium heat, then add the dates, cardamom and quinoa. Cover and simmer for 20 minutes, or until all the liquid has been absorbed. Remove from the heat and leave covered for 5 minutes.

Purée the bananas with the vanilla in a food processor and fold into the cooked quinoa. Spoon the mixture into four 125 ml (4 fl oz) ramekins and seal with plastic wrap. Place each pudding in a steamer and steam for 5 minutes, then remove and serve warm with coconut.

Serves 4

2 cups orange juice

¼ cup fresh dates, finely chopped

½ teaspoon ground cardamom

1 cup quinoa, well rinsed

3 ripe bananas

1 teaspoon natural vanilla extract

2 tablespoons desiccated (dried, shredded) coconut

Creamy millet, apricots and roasted almonds

This luscious millet breakfast will also double as a hearty and satisfying pudding. All you need to do is cool it in a mould, then steam and serve it up warm later on. If you want an extra creamy texture, substitute soy, rice or coconut milk for a cup of the water.

Cook the millet in a dry frying pan over medium heat for 3 minutes, stirring, until lightly browned. Add the fresh and dried apricots, ginger, lemon zest, apple juice, sea salt and 2 cups water.

Bring to the boil, reduce the heat to low then cover and simmer for 12–15 minutes, or until the millet is soft and creamy. Top with the almonds and serve.

Serves 4

1 cup hulled millet, washed and drained

5 fresh apricots or peaches, stones removed and quartered

¼ cup dried apricots or raisins

2 cm (¾ in) knob of ginger, finely chopped

1 teaspoon lemon zest

1 cup apple juice

pinch of sea salt

¼ cup almonds, roasted and roughly chopped

Hot corn cakes
with apple and raisin sauce

This hotcake batter is thicker and denser than regular pancake batter. I've used corn as the filling, but feel free to add grated zucchini (courgette), carrot or shredded spinach – you can even add some spices or chilli if you like a little heat first thing in the morning.

To make the apple and raisin sauce, add the boiling water to the tamarind in a bowl and stir to dissolve before straining through a fine sieve. Combine the strained tamarind, apple, raisins and sea salt with enough water to cover the ingredients in a heavy-based saucepan. Bring to the boil over high heat, then reduce the heat, cover and simmer for 25 minutes, or until the apples have cooked down to a creamy consistency. Transfer to a food processor and purée into a smooth sauce then fold in the lemon zest and set aside.

To prepare the hotcakes, combine the spelt flour, polenta, baking powder and sea salt in a large bowl and make a well in the centre. Beat the eggs and soy milk together in a separate bowl and pour into the centre, gradually working the flour into the egg, while adding 1 cup water. Whisk the batter until smooth, then stir in the onion and corn and refrigerate for 30 minutes.

Heat 1 teaspoon oil in a frying pan over medium heat then add a few small ladles of batter. Cook each hotcake for 3–4 minutes, or until the top side sets and the underside is golden. Gently lift and flip to cook the other side for 2–3 minutes. Serve the hot corn cakes with the sauce.

Makes 12

APPLE AND RAISIN SAUCE

1 cup boiling water
100 g (3½ oz) tamarind
5 jonathan (red) apples, cored, roughly chopped
1 tablespoon raisins
pinch of sea salt
½ teaspoon lemon zest

1 cup unbleached spelt flour
1 cup instant polenta (cornmeal)
2 teaspoons baking powder
1½ teaspoons sea salt
2 eggs
½ cup soy milk
¼ red (Spanish) onion, finely diced
1 corn cob, kernels removed
olive oil, for frying
1 teaspoon freshly ground black pepper
¼ teaspoon chopped chilli

Blueberry muffins

This is my basic muffin recipe: add the wet to the dry, stir and bake. For a tasty variation, replace the apple juice concentrate with barley malt syrup to create a richer tasting muffin with a crispy top. Or, if you like, add some chopped walnuts, almonds or hazelnuts to the mixture just prior to baking.

Preheat the oven to 170°C (340°F/Gas Mark 3). Grease or line a 12-hole standard muffin tin. Combine the spelt flour, polenta, baking powder, bicarbonate of soda and sea salt in a large bowl and make a well in the centre. In another bowl, whisk together the apple juice concentrate, oil, milk and eggs.

Pour the wet ingredients into the dry ingredients and stir to incorporate, then fold through the blueberries and lemon zest. Spoon the mixture into the prepared muffin tin and bake for 25 minutes, or until golden and cooked through when a skewer inserted comes out clean. Serve warm.

Makes 12

1½ cups unbleached spelt flour

1 cup fine polenta (cornmeal)

1 tablespoon baking powder

½ teaspoon bicarbonate of soda (baking soda)

pinch of sea salt

½ cup apple juice concentrate

½ cup macadamia oil or rice bran oil

1½ cups soy milk or buttermilk

2 eggs

150 g (5½ oz) fresh blueberries

zest of 1 lemon

Soups

Soups can be smooth and silky, hot and spicy, thick and wholesome – they can soothe the soul and heal the body.

Miso-style soups are simmered clear stocks fortified with miso paste – a fermented soy and grain paste combined with unrefined sea salt. When simmered as part of a soup, miso develops layers of flavour and depth.

Deliciously creamy soups emerge when seasonal, sweet and colourful vegetables are simmered with onion or leek to create a natural dessert in a bowl. They can be puréed and seasoned with sea salt or miso, then drizzled with ginger juice or topped with citrus zest for some additional excitement.

For that all-embracing soup sensation, try a grain- or bean-based soup, or a blend of both. Remember to soak beans and grains overnight, or cover them with boiling water for at least two hours before cooking.

A soup can have a mind of its own and can change its identity midstream. So, following are a few tips to keep the process simple:

Sauté or 'sweat' your onion, leek, garlic and sea salt to increase sweetness and enhance flavour. A little effort in the beginning will reward you at the end.

Lid on or off? Keeping a lid on aids the sweating process, helping to create a sweeter, richer flavoured soup. So, for a creamy vegetable soup, I tend keep the lid on. When cooking a grain- or bean-style soup I prefer the lid off, which allows the gas to escape from the beans.

A great vegetable stock can be the backbone to a really good tasting soup. If you haven't time to make your own then purchase a good-quality low-salt, organic vegetable stock. Don't use kitchen scraps for making stocks – choose sweet-tasting produce. Try my standard Vegetable Stock recipe (see opposite) – but add and subtract according to what you have to hand or your mood.

I use miso as my everyday flavouring as much as possible. It's the base to my soups when I don't want to use vegetable stock. Miso is such a versatile ingredient – it can be delicate in Asian-style soups or robust and bold in Mediterranean-style soups. Whenever possible I purchase organic, unpasteurised miso and always have at least two varieties to hand: a white (shiro) miso, which has a mellow, sweet flavour and a creamy consistency; and a barley (mugi) miso, which is tan in colour, slightly salty and robust. If you can find an aged miso then you've got a prized flavouring at hand. If you purchase miso in plastic, transfer it to a glass jar and refrigerate – it will last for years. When adding miso to a soup, first spoon the miso into a bowl and dissolve it with a few tablespoons of the soup liquid before pouring it back into the pan.

I've included sea vegetables such as wakame and kombu in many of my soups. These are natural flavour enhancers that have a thickening quality and add minerals to a dish. If you're not used to the flavour of sea vegetables, start with small amounts and increase as you begin to enjoy them.

Don't be afraid to add handfuls of fresh herbs to your soups. Like other produce, herbs have their seasons. I separate them into two categories: soft, spring/summer herbs, such as chervil, coriander (cilantro), parsley, chives and basil, which are delicate and aromatic and are best added at the end of the cooking process; and the more robust autumn/winter range, such as thyme, rosemary and sage, which are hardy and can be added at the beginning of the cooking process.

Finally, if you have a gas cooker, a flame diffuser is vital. Flame diffusers are metal plates shaped like a table tennis bat, designed to disperse and slow a gas flame. They allow thick, grain- or bean-based soups to linger longer on the stove without burning the base. They're also perfect for casseroles.

Basic miso soup

Miso is a pick-me-up soup I enjoy as a winter breakfast, or a light evening meal. This soup is based on a few sliced vegetables in water, enriched with digestive-strengthening miso. White miso is sweet and creamy, while darker miso varieties, such as brown rice and barley miso, are more concentrated, saltier and deeply strengthening. A cup of miso a day keeps depression at bay!

Bring the onion, wakame, shiitake and soaking liquid and 4 cups water to the boil over high heat. Reduce the heat to medium, cover and simmer for 15 minutes. Add the carrot and daikon and simmer for a further 3 minutes. Reduce the heat to very low so that the water stops boiling.

Put the miso in a bowl, pour in some broth and mix until the miso dissolves. Add the diluted miso to the pan with the cabbage or bok choy. Increase the heat and simmer, without boiling, for another 3 minutes. Ladle the soup into bowls, top with spring onion and serve warm.

Serves 4

½ onion, finely sliced

6 cm (2¼ in) piece of wakame, immersed in water for 30 minutes, then sliced finely

3 dried shiitake mushrooms, soaked in 1 cup water for 10 minutes, stems removed and thinly sliced (reserve the soaking water)

½ carrot, cut into fine matchsticks

½ daikon, thinly sliced into half moons

1 tablespoon barley miso

100 g (3½ oz) Chinese cabbage or bok choy (pak choy), sliced into 2 cm (¾ in) pieces

2 tablespoons finely sliced spring onions (scallions)

Vegetable stock

Make your own stock and you'll never go back to the bland supermarket varieties. To add some sweetness, include diced pumpkin or corn kernels. For something a little more robust, add winter herbs, such as thyme or rosemary, or a few garlic cloves.

Bring the ingredients with 5 cups water to the boil in a heavy-based saucepan over high heat. Reduce the heat to medium and simmer for 30 minutes. Strain and allow to cool before you refrigerate and use as needed. This stock will keep in the fridge for 3–4 days, or in the freezer for up to 3 months.

Makes 4 cups

1 onion or leek, cut into wedges or sliced

1 carrot, unpeeled, roughly chopped

3 celery stalks, diced

1 bay leaf

5 flat-leaf (Italian) parsley stems

Creamy split pea soup with bitter greens

Try a bowl of this luscious soup of mushy split peas and wilted bitter leaves and you won't be disappointed. For a heartier meal, serve this soup with crusty cornbread or ladle it over some steamed rice.

Drain the split peas and kombu and add to a saucepan with the bay leaf and the stock or water. Bring to the boil over high heat, skimming the surface scum as it boils, then lower the heat and simmer for 30 minutes, or until the split peas soften.

Meanwhile, heat the oil in a separate saucepan over medium heat and sauté the onion and garlic for 3 minutes, or until softened. Add the carrot, celery and a sprinkling of sea salt to the pan with ½ cup water. Reduce the heat to low, cover and cook for 5 minutes. Add the simmered vegetables and any liquid to the split pea broth midway through the cooking time.

Put the miso in a bowl, pour in some broth and mix until the miso dissolves. Add the diluted miso to the pan with the rocket, dandelion or radicchio and cook for 3 minutes, until wilted. Top with the parsley and serve.

Serves 4

1 cup split green peas, soaked for 2–3 hours with a 3 cm (1¼ in) piece of kombu

1 bay leaf

6 cups Vegetable Stock (page 39) or water

1 tablespoon olive oil

1 onion, diced

½ teaspoon crushed garlic

½ carrot, diced

2 celery stalks, diced

sea salt

1 tablespoon unpasteurised barley or sweet white miso (or a combination)

200 g (7 oz) rocket (arugula), dandelion or radicchio (Italian chicory), chopped

¼ cup flat-leaf (Italian) parsley

Sweet and sour soup with swimming noodles

This has to be one of my all-time favourite soups – it's simple to make, yet is a complete meal in a pot. If you like, substitute fresh Chinese rice noodles for the udon noodles, or prawns (shrimp) instead of the tofu. As it is, though, it will create a soul-soothing meal that will nourish your insides. Serve it piping hot in winter, or at room temperature on a warm day.

Bring 4 cups water, the kombu strips, onion and ginger to the boil in a saucepan over high heat. Reduce the heat to medium–low, cover and simmer for 15 minutes.

Meanwhile, heat the sesame oil in frying pan over medium heat and sauté the tofu cubes for 3–5 minutes, or until lightly browned. Transfer the tofu to the vegetable broth with the carrot and noodles and simmer for 2–3 minutes.

Add the sweet and sour sauce ingredients to the pan with the snow peas and simmer for a further 2–3 minutes. Ladle into bowls and top with spring onion, sesame seeds and drizzle with ginger juice.

Serves 4

Note: Grate a 1 cm (½ in) knob of ginger, place in a muslin cloth (cheesecloth) and squeeze out the juice.

3 cm (1¼ in) piece of kombu, soaked in water for 30 minutes, then cut into 3 mm (⅛ in) strips

1 onion, finely sliced into half moons

3 cm (1¼ in) slice of ginger, cut into fine matchsticks

1 teaspoon dark roasted sesame oil

100 g (3½ oz) firm tofu, cut into 1 cm (½ in) cubes

½ carrot, cut into matchsticks

200 g (7 oz) fresh udon noodles

8 snow peas (mangetout), cut into 3 long strips

2 tablespoons diagonally sliced spring onions (scallions)

2 tablespoons toasted sesame seeds (optional)

1 teaspoon ginger juice (see Note)

SWEET AND SOUR SAUCE

⅓ cup shoyu

2 tablespoons brown rice vinegar

⅓ cup brown rice syrup or barley malt

Cannellini bean and barley soup

This is a super-charged soup with a couple of kissing cousins – a bean and a grain. It's wholesome in every way, with flavours leaning towards southern Italy. This thick, rich soup is seasoned with barley miso, which is my way of adding a stock base flavour without having to make a stock, resulting in a cleaner, lighter tasting soup.

Drain the beans, kombu and barley, and add to a saucepan with the stock or water. Bring to the boil over high heat, then reduce the heat and simmer for 15–20 minutes.

Meanwhile, heat the oil in a separate saucepan over medium heat and sauté the leek for 3 minutes, or until softened. Add the carrot and diced tomatoes to the pan with 3 tablespoons water and a sprinkling of sea salt, cover and simmer over low heat for 15 minutes. Add this mixture to the bean and barley mixture and continue to simmer for a further 15–20 minutes, or until the beans are soft.

Put the miso in a bowl, pour in some broth and mix until the miso dissolves. Add the diluted miso to the pan and simmer for 3 minutes. Just before serving, stir in the sliced olives and top with the basil.

Serves 4

Note: If you're using a strong stock, halve the quantity of miso. Otherwise, simply flavour according to your taste, adding more miso as required.

½ cup dried cannellini beans, soaked overnight in enough water to cover with a 3 cm (1¼ in) piece of kombu

½ cup pearled barley, soaked overnight in enough water to cover

6 cups Vegetable Stock (page 39) or water

1 tablespoon olive oil

½ leek, white part only, finely sliced

½ carrot, diced

2 tomatoes, diced

sea salt

1 tablespoon barley miso

8 pitted black olives, sliced

10 basil leaves, sliced

Rosemary, chickpea and wheat berry soup

This is a truly balanced meal in a saucepan, but it does require some planning and time to cook. The wheat berries give this soup a great chewy texture and can be found in most Middle Eastern grocers or health food stores.

Heat the oil in a heavy-based saucepan over medium heat and sauté the onion, garlic and rosemary for 3 minutes, or until softened. Add the pumpkin, parsnip and celery to the pan with a pinch of sea salt and sauté for 5 minutes.

Drain the chickpeas and wheat berries and slice the kombu and add to the pan with the stock or water. Bring to the boil over high heat, then reduce the heat and simmer, covered, for 40 minutes. Season and stir through the spinach just before serving.

Serves 4

1 tablespoon olive oil

1 onion, diced

1 teaspoon finely sliced garlic

1 teaspoon rosemary leaves

200 g (7 oz) pumpkin, diced

100 g (3½ oz) parsnip, diced

2 celery stalks, diced

sea salt

1 cup dried chickpeas (garbanzo beans), soaked overnight in enough water to cover with a 3 cm (1¼ in) piece of kombu

½ cup wheat berries, soaked overnight in enough water to cover

6 cups Vegetable Stock (page 39) or water

freshly ground black pepper

200 g (7 oz) baby spinach leaves

Sweet corn
and minted green pea soup

This is a soup that simply celebrates the flavours of late summer with deliciously sweet corn and fresh garden peas. It's a creamy, rich and tasty treat.

Heat the sesame oil in a saucepan over medium heat and sauté the onion with a pinch of sea salt for 3 minutes, or until softened. Add the corn kernels and celery and top with the stock or water. Cover the pan and simmer for 7 minutes. Add the peas and cook for a further 5 minutes.

Put the miso in a bowl, pour in some broth and mix until the miso dissolves. Add the diluted miso to the pan and simmer for 3 minutes. Serve topped with mint.

Serves 4

1 teaspoon dark roasted
  sesame oil

1 onion, diced

sea salt

2 corn cobs, kernels removed

2 celery stalks, diced

4 cups Vegetable Stock
  (page 39) or water

300 g (10½ oz) shelled fresh
  green peas

2 tablespoons sweet white miso

1 tablespoon finely sliced
  mint leaves

Lemony leek and cauliflower soup

This is a heartwarming, creamy soup with a satisfying lemon tang – what a great way to welcome spring.

Heat the oil in a saucepan over medium heat and sauté the onion and garlic with a pinch of sea salt for 3 minutes, or until softened. Add the leek, cauliflower and 1 tablespoon water and sauté for 5 minutes. Top with the stock or water, cover and simmer for 15 minutes.

Remove the pan from the heat and add the tofu. Transfer the mixture to a food processor or blender in batches and process until smooth and silky, then return to the pan. Alternatively, process the soup using a hand-held blender.

Put the miso in a bowl, pour in some broth and mix until the miso dissolves. Add the diluted miso to the soup, put the pan back over medium heat and simmer for 3 minutes. Just before serving, stir through the lemon juice and dill.

Serves 4

1 teaspoon olive oil

1 onion, diced

1 garlic clove, crushed

sea salt

2 leeks, white part only, sliced lengthwise, rinsed and finely sliced

300 g (10½ oz) cauliflower florets

4 cups Vegetable Stock (page 39) or water

150 g (5½ oz) silken tofu

2 tablespoons sweet white miso

3 tablespoons lemon juice

1 tablespoon finely chopped dill

Italian fish soup

A well-made fish soup brings out the sunshine. This soup can be approached in two parts – stock one day and the soup recipe the next day – or embraced in one marathon effort. This soup works best with vegetables cut into matchsticks, julienne-style, as they make for a quick cooking time and a light consistency. This is a soup fit for a family feast.

For the fish stock, combine the ingredients together in a large saucepan with 4 litres water. Bring to the boil over high heat, then reduce the heat and simmer for 30 minutes, skimming the surface scum. Strain through a fine sieve and allow to cool.

For the soup, heat 2 tablespoons oil in a heavy-based saucepan over medium heat and sauté the onion, garlic and chilli for 3 minutes, or until softened. Add the carrot, celery and fennel to the pan and sauté for a further 3 minutes. Pour in the wine and allow to evaporate for 1 minute. Add the diced tomatoes and 1.5 litres (51 fl oz) of the fish stock and simmer for 10 minutes to let the flavours come together.

Add the seafood and sea salt to the pan and simmer over low heat for 5 minutes, or until the seafood is cooked through. Just before serving, stir through the basil and drizzle with 1 teaspoon oil.

Serves 6

Note: Store any leftover fish stock in the fridge for 3–4 days or in the freezer for up to 3 months.

FISH STOCK

2 fish carcasses, heads included, rinsed

1 onion, roughly chopped

3 garlic cloves, sliced

1 carrot, roughly chopped

2 celery stalks, roughly chopped

1 bay leaf

1 teaspoon black peppercorns

½ bunch flat-leaf (Italian) parsley stems

2 tablespoons extra virgin olive oil, plus 1 teaspoon, extra, for drizzling

1 onion, finely sliced

1 garlic clove, sliced

¼ chilli, finely sliced (optional)

½ carrot, cut into fine matchsticks

1 celery stalk, cut into fine matchsticks

¼ fennel bulb, finely sliced

½ cup dry white wine

2 × 400 g (14 oz) cans diced tomatoes

250 g (9 oz) assorted seafood, such as snapper, flathead, perch, scallops, prawns (shrimp) and mussels

1 teaspoon sea salt

1 small handful sliced basil leaves

Cream of pumpkin and coconut soup

Welcome autumn's bright orange pumpkins with this Thai-inspired soup. The coconut cream adds a rich silkiness, while the ginger juice adds excitement.

Purée or pound the paste ingredients with ½ cup water in a food processor or with a mortar and pestle until smooth.

Heat a heavy-based saucepan over medium heat and sauté the paste for 3–5 minutes, or until fragrant. Add the pumpkin, lime leaves and 1 cup water to the pan. Simmer for 15 minutes, then add the coconut cream and sea salt and simmer over low heat. Once the pumpkin is soft, remove the pan from the heat and discard the lime leaves. Transfer the mixture to a food processor and process until smooth, then return to the pan. Alternatively, process the soup using a hand-held blender.

Put the pan back over medium heat to warm through. Just before serving, stir through the Thai basil and lemon juice. Serve with the ginger juice drizzled over the top.

Serves 4

Note: Grate a 1 cm (½ in) knob of ginger, place in a muslin cloth (cheesecloth) and squeeze out the juice.

PASTE

1 onion, diced

1 tablespoon finely diced ginger

1 teaspoon diced fresh turmeric or ½ teaspoon ground turmeric

1 tablespoon diced galangal

½ lemongrass stem, white part only, finely chopped

1 garlic clove, crushed

1 small red chilli, sliced (optional)

8 coriander (cilantro) roots, chopped

500 g (1 lb 2 oz) pumpkin, cut into 2 cm (¾ in) cubes

3 kaffir lime leaves

400 ml (14 fl oz) coconut cream

½ teaspoon sea salt

1 tablespoon finely sliced Thai basil leaves

2 teaspoons lemon juice

1 teaspoon ginger juice (see Note)

Red lentil, lemon and coriander soup

This is one of those soups for all seasons and all reasons – it's quick to make, easy to eat and simple to transform into a dip or a thick pasta sauce. Add chilli if you want a little heat and, if you like, a dollop of thick yoghurt or labna for some extra creaminess.

Heat the oil in a heavy-based saucepan over medium heat and sauté the onion and garlic for 3 minutes, or until softened. Add the cumin and turmeric to the pan and sauté for a further 2–3 minutes. Add the carrot and celery with 2 tablespoons water, cover and cook for 3 minutes.

Add the lentils with 5 cups water and simmer for 20 minutes, or until the lentils are tender. Just before serving, season with sea salt, and stir through the lemon juice and coriander.

Serves 4

1 teaspoon olive oil
1 onion, diced
1 garlic clove, crushed
1 teaspoon ground cumin
1 teaspoon ground turmeric
1 carrot, diced
2 celery stalks, diced
1 cup red lentils, well rinsed
sea salt
2 tablespoons lemon juice
1 tablespoon coriander (cilantro) leaves

Salads

If you're used to salads being a mix of cold and raw ingredients then the following recipes are going to come as a bit of a surprise. In this chapter you'll experience some refreshingly new ways of creating salads using grains, beans, soy foods, vegetables and noodles combined with mouth-watering, high enzyme dressings to create nutritious and satisfying dishes. All of the salads in this section can be used as side dishes and many of them as stand alone meals, which can be eaten either cold or warm.

I try to think of salads as a four-part symphony comprising a base, body, dressing and garnish. The base is often the principal ingredient of the salad, such as cooked barley grains, cannellini beans or buckwheat noodles. The base ingredient dictates if the salad is to become a wholesome winter meal, or a light-hearted summer side dish.

The body is then a group of friends – vegetable accompaniments – that come along to support the base, such as blanched carrot batons, asparagus spears and fresh peas.

Part three of the symphony is the dressing, which is designed to bring all the ingredients together with flavour and texture. The dressing works closely with the next player – the garnish. These two can sway the flavour of your salad into Mediterranean seas or Asian territories. Garnishes can be as simple as lemon or lime zest, fresh herbs or toasted nuts.

One more tip before we get started: if you create a grain salad, such as one with a couscous base, and then add a bean product, such as chickpeas (garbanzo beans), you are venturing into creating a hearty, protein-packed meal, which is much more than a side dish.

Salads
Salads

Baby leek and asparagus salad with miso dressing

Welcome spring with this crisp vegetable salad. If you like, serve the vegetables warm with the dressing.

Snap the asparagus at the base and discard the woody ends. Blanch the asparagus and leeks separately in boiling water until *al dente*, then refresh under cold running water. Drain well. Cut the asparagus in half on a diagonal.

Warm the dressing ingredients in a saucepan over low heat for 2–3 minutes. Remove from the saucepan and cool.

Arrange the leeks and asparagus on a platter and spoon the dressing over the top. Sprinkle with the sesame seeds.

Serves 4

1 bunch baby asparagus

8 baby leeks, trimmed, cut into 6 cm (2¼ in) lengths

3 tablespoons toasted sesame seeds

DRESSING

3 tablespoons white miso

1 teaspoon dijon mustard

1 tablespoon rice vinegar

1 tablespoon mirin

2 tablespoons lemon juice

Millet tabbouleh

This is a great year-round grain salad, which I've adapted from a recipe in Rebecca Wood's book *The Splendid Grain*. Turn this into a complete meal by adding a can of cooked chickpeas (garbanzo beans), or some fried tempeh croutons.

Bring the millet, turmeric and 2 cups water to the boil in a saucepan over high heat. Reduce the heat to low and simmer, covered, for 20 minutes. Allow to sit for 5 minutes, covered, then spoon out into a large bowl. Drizzle with some oil to separate the grains and allow to cool.

To make the dressing, whisk the garlic, oil, vinegar and lemon juice together in a bowl. Season to taste with sea salt and freshly ground black pepper.

Combine the millet, cucumber, tomato, olive, parsley, mint and walnuts in a bowl. Just before serving pour over the dressing and mix to combine.

Serves 4

1 cup hulled millet, rinsed in a fine sieve

½ teaspoon ground turmeric

extra virgin olive oil

½ teaspoon sea salt

1 cucumber, cut into 2 cm (¾ in) cubes

100 g (3½ oz) cherry tomatoes, halved

10 pitted black olives, sliced

3 tablespoons roughly chopped flat-leaf (Italian) parsley

3 tablespoons roughly chopped mint

50 g (1¾ oz) roughly chopped roasted walnuts

DRESSING

1 garlic clove, crushed

3 tablespoons extra virgin olive oil

1 tablespoon white wine vinegar

1 tablespoon lemon juice

sea salt and freshly ground black pepper

Bean salad with lemon and parsley dressing

I love bean salads – and this is a particular favourite. This dish is a wholesome meal loaded with protein and made light and digestible with vegetables and a citrus dressing. I often can't wait for the beans to cool down so I end up eating them warm. Feel free to take a shortcut and use some organic canned beans, or substitute with other beans or legumes, such as chickpeas (garbanzo beans).

Drain the cannellini beans and kombu and add to a heavy-based saucepan with enough water to cover. Bring to the boil, uncovered, and simmer for 30–40 minutes, or until tender. Drain and transfer to a large serving bowl.

Meanwhile, preheat the oven to 200°C (400°F/Gas Mark 6) and roast the capsicum for 5–10 minutes, or until the skin is black and blistered. Transfer to a plastic bag and allow to sweat for 30 minutes before removing and discarding the skin and seeds. Chop the flesh into 1 cm (½ in) cubes and add to the bowl.

Blanch the carrot and peas separately in boiling water until just cooked. Refresh under cold running water and add to the bowl with the beans and capsicum.

To make the dressing, purée all the dressing ingredients in a food processor until smooth. Mix the dressing through the bean mixture and serve.

Serves 4

1 cup dried cannellini beans, soaked overnight in enough water to cover with a 3 cm (1¼ in) piece of kombu

1 red capsicum (pepper)

½ carrot, diced

200 g (7 oz) fresh peas

DRESSING

⅓ cup extra virgin olive oil

3 tablespoons lemon juice

1 tablespoon rice vinegar

1 garlic clove, crushed

1 teaspoon dijon mustard

½ cup roughly chopped flat-leaf (Italian) parsley

zest of 1 lemon

¼ teaspoon sea salt

Couscous, chickpea and avocado salad

Couscous is a nutritious grain and makes a super-fast, hearty meal when combined with canned chickpeas (garbanzo beans).

Bring 1 cup water to the boil in a saucepan over high heat. Add the couscous, chickpeas and turmeric with a pinch of sea salt, bring back to a rolling boil, cover and simmer for 3 minutes. Remove from the heat and leave, with the lid on, for 5 minutes before spooning into a large bowl. Gently separate the grains with a fork and allow to cool.

To make the lemon–tahini dressing, process all the dressing ingredients with 1 tablespoon water in a food processor until smooth.

Add the avocado, rocket, lime zest and pumpkin seeds to the couscous and chickpea mixture. Gently mix to combine and spoon the dressing over the top to serve.

Serves 4

1 cup couscous

400 g (14 oz) can organic chickpeas (garbanzo beans), rinsed and drained

1 teaspoon ground turmeric

sea salt

1 avocado, sliced

100 g (3½ oz) rocket (arugula), chopped

zest of 1 lime

2 tablespoons toasted pumpkin seeds (pepitas)

LEMON–TAHINI DRESSING

½ cup hulled tahini

⅔ cup lemon juice

1 teaspoon honey

1 teaspoon umeboshi paste

2 cm (¾ in) knob of ginger, finely grated

½ cup roughly chopped flat-leaf (Italian) parsley

¼ teaspoon sea salt

¼ teaspoon freshly ground black pepper

Broccoli and green bean salad with lemon tofu mayo

This is a blanched vegetable salad that I've been making for years. I add the red cabbage for flavour and colour and change the dressing from time to time. This recipe includes my version of a clean tasting, egg-free mayo.

Blanch the broccoli and green beans separately in boiling water until *al dente*. Refresh under cold running water and drain. Set aside.

Combine the cabbage and parsley in a bowl with the vinegar and a pinch of sea salt. Mix well and marinate for at least 30 minutes – the cabbage will begin to pickle.

To make the lemon tofu mayo, purée all the ingredients in a food processor until smooth.

To assemble, layer the broccoli and beans with the red cabbage and parsley pickle and top with the mayo.

Serves 4

250 g (9 oz) broccoli florets

250 g (9 oz) green beans, trimmed

100 g (3½ oz) red cabbage, finely shredded

2 tablespoons roughly chopped flat-leaf (Italian) parsley

1 tablespoon umeboshi vinegar

sea salt

LEMON TOFU MAYO

300 g (10½ oz) silken tofu

1 tablespoon extra virgin olive oil

2 tablespoons lemon juice

2 teaspoons lemon zest

1 tablespoon diced preserved lemon

1 teaspoon dijon mustard

¼ teaspoon ground turmeric

¼ teaspoon sea salt

¼ teaspoon freshly ground black pepper

2 teaspoons white miso

2 teaspoons brown rice vinegar

Raw slaw

This is a fantastically fresh and crisp salad – enjoy it as a refreshing side dish to a heavy meal. If you like, prepare it ahead of time as it will keep fresh in the refrigerator for up to three days.

Combine the cabbage, carrot, celery, apple, radish and mint in a large bowl. Sprinkle the sea salt over and mix thoroughly with your hands, using a kneading motion. Place the ingredients in a pickle press or cover with a plate and weigh down with a heavy object for 1–2 hours.

Meanwhile, roast the walnuts in a preheated 170°C (340°F/ Gas Mark 3) oven for 7 minutes, or until golden. Allow to cool, then roughly chop and set aside.

Remove the ingredients from the pickle press and squeeze out the excess liquid. If the mixture is too salty, rinse quickly under cold water in a fine sieve. Transfer to a serving bowl, fold in the roasted walnuts, shiso leaves and raisins and pour on the brown rice vinegar and mirin. Mix well and serve.

Serves 4

200 g (7 oz) green cabbage, finely shredded

200 g (7 oz) red cabbage, finely shredded

½ carrot, cut into fine matchsticks

1 celery stalk, thinly sliced on the diagonal

1 green apple, finely sliced

5 red radishes, finely sliced

2 tablespoons roughly chopped mint leaves

2 teaspoons sea salt

50 g (1¾ oz) walnuts

1 small handful shiso leaves

30 g (1¼ oz) raisins

2 teaspoons brown rice vinegar

2 teaspoons mirin

Quinoa, pumpkin and orange salad

This quinoa salad is a happy spring affair with lots of sweetness and a dash of sunshine.

Bring the quinoa, 1½ cups water and a pinch of sea salt to the boil in a saucepan over high heat. Reduce the heat, cover and simmer for 12 minutes, or until all the water has been absorbed. Allow to cool slightly before spooning into a large bowl to cool completely.

Heat the oil in a saucepan over low heat and sauté the onion with a pinch of sea salt for 7 minutes, or until caramelised. Add the vinegar and orange juice and simmer for 2 minutes. Add the pumpkin and heat through for 3 minutes. Remove from the heat and allow to cool slightly. Add the mixture to the quinoa with the mint, pumpkin seeds, orange zest and season with sea salt and freshly ground black pepper. Mix well and serve as a warm salad, or leave to cool completely.

Serves 4

1 cup quinoa, rinsed in a fine sieve

sea salt

1 tablespoon extra virgin olive oil

1½ brown onions, diced

1½ tablespoons white wine vinegar

2 tablespoons orange juice

200 g (7 oz) pumpkin, peeled and grated

2 tablespoons torn mint leaves

2 tablespoons toasted pumpkin seeds (pepitas)

1 teaspoon orange zest

freshly ground black pepper

Fennel, greens and orange salad

This is a mouth-puckering salad that refreshes and arouses the taste buds. I've balanced the bitterness of the salad leaves with sweet oranges and balsamic vinegar. Eat it with a hearty Sunday lunch.

Separate the lettuce and radicchio leaves and immerse in a large bowl of water. Wash each leaf individually, then dry in a salad spinner. Cut the salad leaves into bite-sized pieces and place in a salad bowl. Add the rocket, onion, fennel, orange segments and sliced olives.

To make the dressing, whisk together the ingredients in a bowl. Just before serving, pour the dressing over the greens and toss gently to combine.

Serves 4

1 head of witlof (chicory/ Belgian endive)

1 head of radicchio (Italian chicory)

200 g (7 oz) rocket (arugula)

½ red (Spanish) onion, finely sliced

½ fennel bulb, finely sliced

2 oranges, segmented

10 pitted green olives, sliced

ORANGE DRESSING

3 tablespoons fresh orange juice

3 tablespoons extra virgin olive oil

1 teaspoon balsamic vinegar

¼ teaspoon sea salt

¼ teaspoon freshly ground black pepper

Soba noodle salad
with creamy avocado dressing

Noodle salads are simple to prepare and one of the easiest foods to digest. The longer the dressing sits with the noodles the yummier they become. If you love garlic and would like to give this salad an extra kick, grate a clove into the dressing.

Cook the noodles using the 'shock' method (see page 146). Refresh under cold running water, then drain and set aside.

Blanch the snow peas and peas separately in boiling water until *al dente*. Refresh under cold running water. Finely slice the snow peas.

For the dressing, peel the avocado, remove the stone and spoon the flesh into a food processor. Add the remaining dressing ingredients and purée until creamy and smooth. Spoon the dressing over the noodles. Add the snow peas, peas and cucumber and toss to combine. Serve immediately or allow to marinate for 30 minutes if time permits.

Serves 4

250 g (9 oz) buckwheat (soba) noodles

200 g (7 oz) snow peas (mangetout), trimmed

1 cup shelled peas

½ cup finely sliced cucumber

DRESSING

1 avocado

2 tablespoons lemon juice

2 tablespoons extra virgin olive oil

¼ teaspoon sea salt

¼ teaspoon freshly ground black pepper

1 teaspoon roughly chopped dill

pinch of chilli powder

Grains

Wholegrains have long been revered across the globe. They are power-packed, life-sustaining, nutritious foods containing protein, vitamins, minerals, carbohydrates, fats and fibre. Wholegrains are seeds loaded with nutrition, which if planted and sprouted have the ability to become plants, multiplying themselves to provide even more food.

My first experience with grains was a disaster. Millet, quinoa and amaranth all looked alike (and I was sure that I'd bought bird seed). I followed the recipe: wash, add water, stir and cook. Out came a dull, tasteless mush. After many more disasters down the track, wholegrains are now one of my daily staples. Since my first encounter I've gone on to learn that each grain has its own inherent identity, particular taste and cooking method.

We all intuit that grains must be good for us, that they are a natural wholefood containing good levels of fibre and nutrients and that somehow we'd like to start a romance with grains. But we're often unsure how to approach them. As with all good things, start slowly, have a strategy and a plan B.

Following are the do's of romancing the grain:

Buy small amounts, such as 500 g (1 lb 2 oz) packets, and search for the best-quality grains. Try organic foods stores or Mediterranean grocers.

Store grains in glass jars, in a cool, dry and preferably dark spot. Make sure you label the jars – many grains look similar.

Measure the quantity you're about to use and rinse thoroughly to remove dust and any husks. Also, measure the water quantity correctly before cooking.

Use heavy-based stainless steel or cast-iron saucepans or deep frying pans with tight-fitting lids. If you have a gas cooker, have a flame diffuser at hand for slow cooking.

Add unrefined sea salt while the grain is cooking to enhance the flavour and help alkalise the grain.

Grains are a blank canvas and require a lot of flavouring. Add oils such as extra virgin olive or sesame and then splash with rice vinegar, champagne vinegar or freshly squeezed lemon juice. Feel free to add some soft herbs at the end of cooking, such as parsley, coriander (cilantro) or basil leaves.

A grain-based meal can become a complete meal by adding a soy product, such as tofu or tempeh, or beans. Grains and beans are a principal food for many cultures around the world, making them a great comfort food.

If you've got a weak digestion, soak your grains the night before. That is, rinse them as usual then soak in the required amount of water as listed in the recipe. The next day cook the grain along with the soaking water. Soaking the grain the night before also quickens the cooking time.

Another great tip is to chew your grains. Try and make the meal into a liquid before gulping it down. This will help you digest them more easily.

Dry-roasting grains such as brown rice, millet, whole spelt and whole rye will help to crack the shell, accentuate the flavour and reduce the cooking time. To do this, take a heavy-based saucepan, add the required quantity of grain and place over a medium heat and stir continuously until the grains become golden and a toasty nutty smell is released. Add liquid and continue to cook, or cool and store in a jar for later.

Grains Grain

Simple polenta

Polenta takes practice. I sometimes add chopped onion while it's cooking and stir in a couple of tablespoons of chopped parsley just before serving it as a side dish. The leftovers can be set in a baking tray to be grilled (broiled) later. Work with the consistency: if it's a little thick add more water; if it's too thin, stir in some more polenta.

2 teaspoons sea salt

1 cup coarse polenta (cornmeal)

1 tablespoon extra virgin olive oil

Bring 3 cups water and the sea salt to the boil in a heavy-based saucepan over high heat. Whisk in the polenta, being careful not to be splashed. Reduce the heat to low, cover with a lid and simmer for 30–40 minutes, stirring occasionally, or until the polenta comes off the sides easily.

Stir in the oil and serve warm. Alternatively, set in an oiled dish until cold then cut into slices and grill (broil) or fry.

Makes 3½ cups

Polenta and broccoli slice with a creamy pumpkin topping

This recipe has long been a favourite of mine – I often take it along to parties when there are a lot of people to feed. Fortunately, it's easy to prepare and can be made the night before. Serve slices either cool or warm, as a main meal or a starter.

Bring 3 cups water to the boil in a saucepan over high heat and add the corn kernels, onion and a teaspoon of sea salt. Stir in the polenta, reduce the heat to low, cover with a lid and simmer for 30–40 minutes, stirring occasionally, or until the polenta comes off the sides easily. If the polenta thickens early, stir in some more water. Stir in the parsley and pour the mixture into a lightly oiled 16 x 21 cm (6 x 8 in) baking dish. Arrange the broccoli florets over the top of the polenta.

For the topping, steam the pumpkin and onion with a pinch of sea salt in a steamer for 15 minutes, or until soft. Transfer to a food processor and purée until smooth. Add the tahini, ginger juice and orange zest to the processor and purée until smooth and creamy. Pour the mixture over the broccoli and polenta and allow it to set in the refrigerator for about 30 minutes. You can serve this dish at room temperature as a slice, or bake it at 170°C (340°F/Gas Mark 3) for 15–20 minutes, or until lightly browned, for a more wintry meal.

Serves 4

Note: Grate a 1 cm (½ in) knob of ginger and place into a muslin cloth (cheesecloth) and squeeze out the juice.

1 corn cob, kernels removed

1 onion, diced

sea salt

1 cup polenta (cornmeal)

2 tablespoons finely chopped flat-leaf (Italian) parsley

250 g (9 oz) broccoli florets, blanched and sliced in half

PUMPKIN TOPPING

500 g (1 lb 2 oz) pumpkin, peeled and cut into large chunks

1 onion, cut into wedges

sea salt

2 tablespoons hulled tahini

1 teaspoon ginger juice (see Note)

1 teaspoon orange zest

Millet and cauliflower mash

This is an all-time favourite at our place, especially at the first sign of winter. Make it as creamy as you like by adding a little more tahini or olive oil. I love it served with Sweet and Sour Tempeh (page 135) and blanched green beans. Leftover mash is sensational refried the following day.

Heat half the oil in a deep heavy-based saucepan over medium heat and sauté the onion, garlic and a pinch of sea salt for 3–4 minutes, or until softened. Add the millet and sauté for 2–3 minutes. Add the cauliflower, stock or water and sea salt. Bring to the boil, cover and simmer over low heat for 30 minutes, or until the millet has no crunch to it when you bite. Mash the millet and cauliflower mixture well. Add the remaining oil and tahini to achieve a smooth consistency. Stir in the parsley and serve.

Serves 4

Note: Avoid unhulled millet as it will not soften.

2 tablespoons extra virgin olive oil

1 onion, diced

2 garlic cloves, crushed

sea salt

1 cup hulled millet, washed (see Note)

400 g (14 oz) cauliflower florets

3 cups Vegetable Stock (page 39) or water

½ teaspoon sea salt

2 tablespoons hulled tahini

2 tablespoons finely chopped flat-leaf (Italian) parsley

Steamed millet

To create a more flavoursome grain, dry roast the millet in a pan until it browns slightly or begins to pop, then add the water and continue to cook. Millet is a great substitute for couscous. Serve it as a side dish with some Sweet and Sour Sauce (page 198) or Carrot Butter (page 199).

Rinse the millet in a fine sieve then bring the millet, 2 cups water and a pinch of sea salt to the boil in a small saucepan over high heat. Reduce the heat to low, cover and simmer for 20 minutes, or until all the water has been absorbed. Leave to rest, covered, for 5 minutes before spooning out.

Makes 3½ cups

1 cup hulled millet
sea salt

Quinoa, beetroot and almond pilaf

A simple fast food, quinoa is stacked with protein and is easily digested. Serve it warm with some steamed greens and grilled (broiled) fish, or cold in your lunchbox with some roasted vegetables or chicken.

Heat half the oil in a heavy-based saucepan over medium heat and sauté the onion with a pinch of sea salt for 2–3 minutes, or until softened. Add the beetroot and celery and sauté for 1–2 minutes. Spread the vegetables evenly over the base of the saucepan and top with the quinoa. Add the stock or water and ¼ teaspoon sea salt and bring to the boil. Reduce the heat to low, cover and simmer for 25 minutes, or until the quinoa is cooked. Remove from the heat and leave, covered, for 5 minutes. Stir in the remaining oil, pomegranate molasses, orange zest, coriander and toasted almonds. Serve warm.

Serves 4

2 tablespoons extra virgin olive oil

2 red (Spanish) onions, diced

sea salt

1 beetroot (beet), diced

1 celery stalk, diced

1 cup quinoa, rinsed in a fine sieve

1½ cups Vegetable Stock (page 39) or water

2 tablespoons pomegranate molasses

1 teaspoon orange zest

2 tablespoons roughly chopped coriander (cilantro)

¼ cup roasted and sliced almonds

Steamed quinoa

This versatile grain can be transformed into a pilaf or serve it simply with some greens or a bean dish

Bring the quinoa, 1½ cups water and a pinch of sea salt to the boil in a heavy-based saucepan over high heat. Reduce the heat to low, cover and simmer for 15 minutes, or until all the water has been absorbed. Leave to rest, covered, for 5 minutes before spooning out.

Makes 3½ cups

1 cup quinoa, rinsed in a fine sieve

sea salt

Grain and bean combo

This is my version of a special five-grain dish that has its origins in Korea. Tradition has it that if eaten on the first full moon of the year it guarantees great luck and good fortune for the upcoming year. Try varying the grains and use up what's in the pantry before buying more ingredients. Make it your meal by adding a dash of shoyu, sliced spring onion (scallion) and some toasted black sesame seeds.

¼ cup chickpeas (garbanzo beans)
¼ cup green lima (butter) beans
¼ cup kidney beans
2 cm (¾ in) length of kombu
½ cup jasmine rice
¼ cup hulled millet
¼ teaspoon sea salt

Combine the chickpeas, lima beans, kidney beans and kombu with 2 cups hot water in a saucepan and allow to sit for 2 hours. Meanwhile, combine the jasmine rice and millet in a bowl with 2 cups hot water and allow to sit for 2 hours.

Drain the barley and beans, discard the water and cover with fresh water in a saucepan. Bring to the boil over high heat, then reduce the heat and simmer for up to 40 minutes, or until the barley and beans are cooked.

Drain the rice and millet and keep the soaking liquid. Combine the cooked beans with the uncooked rice and millet in a large saucepan with the sea salt and 1½ cups of the rice and millet soaking liquid. Bring to a strong boil, then reduce the heat to low, cover and simmer for 10 minutes, or until all the grains are cooked. Lightly scoop out with a spoon and serve warm.

Serves 4

Carrot and buckwheat patties with cranberry chilli chutney

Buckwheat is the heartiest of all the grains – it creates wholesome sustenance with slow-release energy. In fact, buckwheat and buckwheat noodles (soba) are the preferred food of Japanese sumo wrestlers – so make it when you're in need of a real top up.

To make the chutney, heat the oil in a saucepan over medium heat and sauté the garlic, ginger and chilli for 3 minutes, or until fragrant and slightly golden. Add the onion with a pinch of salt and 2 tablespoons water and sauté for 3 minutes. Add the capsicum, cranberries, vinegar, barley malt and cranberry juice and simmer over low heat for 15 minutes, or until it becomes a thickened chutney. Serve warm or leave to cool and refrigerate in a glass jar.

For the patties, dry-fry the buckwheat in a frying pan over medium heat for 3–4 minutes, or until slightly golden, then set aside. Heat the oil in a large saucepan over medium heat and sauté the onion, garlic, ginger, cumin and turmeric for 3 minutes. Add the carrots and sauté for a further 2 minutes. Add the roasted buckwheat, 2½ cups water and the sea salt to the pan, bring to the boil, then reduce the heat and simmer over low heat for 12 minutes, or until all the liquid has been absorbed. Remove from the heat, cover and leave to stand for 3–5 minutes.

Spoon into a bowl and allow to cool slightly before adding the chopped hazelnuts and herbs. Shape into 8 patties and dust with the polenta. Heat the extra oil in a frying pan over medium heat and cook the patties for 2–3 minutes on each side. Serve with the cranberry chilli chutney on the side or spooned over the top.

Makes 8

CRANBERRY CHILLI CHUTNEY

1 teaspoon extra virgin olive oil

1 garlic clove, crushed

1 teaspoon finely chopped ginger

1 small chilli, seeds removed, finely chopped

½ red (Spanish) onion, diced

¼ red capsicum (pepper), diced

1 cup fresh or frozen cranberries

3 tablespoons apple cider vinegar

1 tablespoon barley malt or rice syrup

1 cup cranberry juice

1 cup unroasted buckwheat groats (kasha)

1 tablespoon olive oil, plus 1 tablespoon, extra, for frying

½ onion, diced

1 garlic clove, crushed

2 teaspoons finely chopped ginger

1 teaspoon ground cumin

½ teaspoon ground turmeric

1 carrot, diced

¼ teaspoon sea salt

¼ cup roasted, chopped hazelnuts

¼ cup chopped mint leaves

¼ cup chopped coriander (cilantro) leaves

½ cup fine polenta (cornmeal)

Brown rice with corn, peas and mint

This simple brown rice dish is transformed with pearls of sweet corn and fresh peas. Serve it with some homemade baked beans or a tofu or tempeh dish. The following day, turn leftovers into rice balls for your lunchbox, by rolling them in sesame seeds and baking them in the oven.

Bring the rice, sea salt and 2 cups water to the boil in a heavy-based saucepan over medium–high heat. Reduce the heat to medium–low, cover and simmer for 40–50 minutes, or until the liquid is absorbed and the rice is tender, adding the corn kernels in the last 7 minutes of the cooking time. Allow tiny vent holes to appear in the grain as it boils and do not disturb as it cooks evenly. If the liquid evaporates and the grains are still hard, add more water and continue cooking until the grains become tender. Allow to rest for 3 minutes before spooning out into a large bowl. Stir in the peas, mint, oil and lemon juice and serve warm.

Serves 4

1 cup organic or biodynamic short-grain brown rice, washed thoroughly

¼ teaspoon sea salt

1 corn cob, kernels removed

1 cup freshly shelled peas, blanched

3 tablespoons finely sliced mint leaves

1 tablespoon extra virgin olive oil

2 tablespoons lemon juice

Steamed brown rice

The size of your saucepan, the age of the rice and grain size will dictate how your rice will cook. Practice makes perfect rice. Buy a heavy-based saucepan and invest in a flame diffuser (if you have a gas stove) to prevent burnt rice.

Rinse the rice in water 2–3 times, or until the water runs clear. Put the rice in a heavy-based saucepan with a pinch of sea salt and 2 cups water for short-grain rice or 1½ cups water for medium- and long-grain rice. Bring to the boil, then reduce the heat, cover and simmer for 50 minutes, or until all the water has been absorbed. Remove from the heat and leave, covered, for 5 minutes before eating.

Makes 2½ cups

1 cup short-, medium- or long-grain brown rice

sea salt

Farro and three mushroom ragout

This dish will soon become an autumn favourite, especially if you've managed to forage for your own wild mushrooms or get your hands on some excellent quality dried mushrooms. If you like, substitute the farro with brown rice, barley or wheat berries in this dish.

Drain the shiitake and porcini mushrooms, keeping the soaking liquid. Remove the woody stems and finely slice the caps; set aside.

Heat half the oil in a large saucepan over medium heat and sauté the garlic for 2 minutes. Add the sage and sauté for 2–3 minutes, until the leaves change colour, then add the onion and a pinch of sea salt and sauté for 5 minutes. Add the celery, sliced dried mushrooms, farro and wine to the pan and sauté for 3–5 minutes, or until the wine has almost evaporated. Add the 5 cups of mushroom soaking liquid with 1 teaspoon sea salt. Bring to the boil, then reduce the heat, cover and simmer for 30 minutes, or until the farro is tender. You can allow any excess liquid to evaporate by leaving the lid off once cooked.

Heat the remaining oil in a frying pan over high heat and sauté the button mushrooms for 3 minutes, or until golden brown. Add the parsley and combine before folding the mushroom mixture through the cooked farro. Add a good dollop of sour cream and the freshly ground black pepper before serving warm.

Serves 4

½ cup dried shiitake mushrooms, soaked overnight in 2½ cups water

½ cup dried porcini mushrooms, soaked overnight in 2½ cups water

2 tablespoons olive oil

2 garlic cloves, finely sliced

5 sage leaves

1 onion, finely sliced

sea salt

2 celery stalks, diced

2 cups farro, soaked overnight with enough water to cover, drained

½ cup dry white wine

8 button mushrooms, cut into quarters

2 tablespoons finely chopped flat-leaf (Italian) parsley

¼–½ cup sour cream or mascarpone

½ teaspoon freshly ground black pepper

Beans & lentils

Beans and lentils are a great addition to everyday feasting as they're nourishing, versatile and flavoursome. You've eaten them, I bet, in your favourite hummus, as dahl at your local Indian restaurant, or maybe refried in a cheesy Mexican taco.

These humble foods have nourished millions with their rich and substantial texture and subtle flavours. They are the 'meat' of any vegetarian meal, providing satisfaction to the body and abundant goodness, without the added fat.

Beans and lentils provide a slow release of energy and, when combined with grains, create a complete protein meal. They are high in fibre and recommended as part of a balanced diet the world over. If that wasn't enough to get you inspired, beans and lentils are also incredibly cheap and easy to prepare.

You can find all sorts of colourful and exotic beans to match your mood in Middle Eastern stores, Italian grocers, Asian grocers and health food shops.

When it comes to cooking, beans and lentils fall into two categories: those that need soaking and those that don't.

Some examples of the 'no need to soak' varieties include red lentils, brown lentils, split green peas and mung beans. These ready-to-cook varieties, which are, incidentally, lower in fat than the soaking varieties, make quick and easy soups, dips and loafs.

Beans and lentils that require soaking before cooking include lima (butter) beans, borlotti (cranberry) beans, chickpeas (garbanzo beans), cannellini beans, adzuki beans, black beans and pinto beans. The soaking varieties tend to be larger than no-soak beans and lentils and make for a wholesome, hearty meal.

To prepare cooking with beans and lentils that require soaking, first start by sifting through and removing any small stones. Rinse then soak them and watch any skins and twigs rise to the top; discard them.

Soak the beans with a 3 cm (1¼ in) piece of kombu for a minimum of six to eight hours before you cook them. Adding seaweed to soaking beans helps to soften them and release any unwanted gas, which makes eating beans uncomfortable. Kombu also helps mineralise the bean dish by adding calcium, iron and other trace elements. After this soaking period your beans will be ready to use in your recipe.

If you've forgotten to soak your beans, or you just don't have the time, you can try the quick cook method: cover your beans with cold water, bring them to a rapid boil over high heat then take off the heat and leave, covered, for about 2 hours before using them.

When you're ready to begin cooking the beans, always discard the soaking water and add clean, fresh water. Boil the beans over high heat and remove any scum that rises to the surface with a ladle or spoon. Continue this process for about 10 minutes and then cover with a lid if required.

Make sure your beans are thoroughly cooked and not *al dente*, otherwise they'll continue to cook in your gut. Allow beans to cool in their cooking liquid before serving. Beans always taste better the following day and freeze well – so go ahead and cook double the amount. Salting beans should always be done at the end of the cooking process as the salt inhibits the bean from softening, creating potential dinner disasters.

Beans are already filled with flavour but become more exciting when cooked with or added to vegetables. They tend to contain a fattiness that is made lighter and more digestible by adding something citrusy or vinegary at the end of the cooking process. Indian, Lebanese and Moroccan bean dishes tend to include a few drops of lemon juice, lime juice or rice vinegar in the final stages to bring all the flavours together and help create a potful of harmony.

For those who haven't the time to soak and cook beans from scratch, go ahead and stock your pantry with some great-quality organic canned beans. They are such an amazing staple to have around and they allow you to create a sustaining meal in minutes. Make sure you rinse them before using and always taste to check their salt quantity and adjust your salt use accordingly.

Lastly, start a habit of chewing beans well, as this will make them much more digestible and easeful on the gut.

eans & lentils
Beans & lentils

Black beans with mango salsa, tofu sour cream and avocado dip

This is a spiced Mexican bean dish served with a variety of toppings. Serve warm over some plain polenta (cornmeal) or scoop up with corn (tortilla) chips.

To make the mango salsa, combine all the ingredients in a bowl and season with sea salt. Refrigerate until ready to use.

To make the tofu sour cream, place the ingredients in a food processor and process until smooth. Adjust the seasoning to taste, and refrigerate until ready to use.

To make the avocado dip, place all of the ingredients in a food processor and process until creamy. (You can also do this using a mortar and pestle and pounding until smooth.) Refrigerate until ready to use.

Drain the black beans and place in a heavy-based saucepan with 4½ cups water. Add the bay leaf and bring to the boil, then reduce the heat to low and simmer for 30–45 minutes, skimming the surface to remove any scum, or until the beans are tender. Drain and reserve the cooking liquid.

Heat the oil in a frying pan over medium heat, add the onion and sauté for 3 minutes, or until softened. Add the garlic, chilli, thyme, cumin and salt and sauté for 2 minutes. Stir in the cooked beans and sherry vinegar and continue to cook, adding some of the bean cooking liquid if the mixture becomes too dry. Mash to create a creamy dip consistency using a potato masher. Adjust the seasoning and keep warm.

Serve the refried beans, mango salsa, tofu sour cream and avocado dip in bowls with lots of corn chips.

Serves 4

MANGO SALSA
1 ripe mango, peeled and cut into 2 cm (¾ in) cubes

1 orange, peeled and sliced into rounds then quartered

¼ green chilli, finely chopped

1 tablespoon roughly chopped coriander (cilantro) leaves

juice of 1 lime

sea salt

TOFU SOUR CREAM
300 g (10½ oz) silken tofu

2 tablespoons olive oil

1 teaspoon rice syrup

2 tablespoons lemon juice

½ teaspoon sweet white miso

sea salt and freshly ground black pepper

AVOCADO DIP
1 ripe avocado, diced

1 garlic clove, crushed

1 tablespoon extra virgin olive oil

1 teaspoon ground cumin

2 tablespoons lime juice

sea salt and freshly ground black pepper

cayenne pepper (optional)

2 cups dried black beans, soaked overnight in water to cover with a 3 cm (1¼ in) piece of kombu

1 bay leaf

2 tablespoons olive oil

½ onion, diced

2 garlic cloves, crushed

1 small chilli, seeded and sliced

½ teaspoon dried thyme

1 teaspoon ground cumin

½ teaspoon sea salt

2 tablespoons sherry vinegar

Persian red lentil and olive casserole

This red lentil recipe was given to me by a dear friend, Jane Seymour of Mount Zero Olive Company. Showcasing Persian red lentils and olives in the same dish, it has a wonderful Mediterranean flavour, is filling and also tastes delightful as leftovers (if there's any left!).

Heat 1 tablespoon oil in a heavy-based saucepan over medium heat, add the onion and garlic and sauté for 3 minutes, or until softened. Add the carrot, thyme, celery and sweet potato, and sauté for 5 minutes, or until slightly brown and softened. Add the lentils, stock and bay leaves. Cover the pan, reduce the heat to low and simmer for 30 minutes, or until the lentils are cooked. Season with the sea salt and freshly ground black pepper and stir through the sliced olives and remaining oil.

Serve the lentils over some Steamed Millet (page 74) or with a slice of toasted sourdough.

Serves 6

- 2 tablespoons extra virgin olive oil
- 1 red (Spanish) onion, cut into wedges
- 2 garlic cloves, crushed
- 1 carrot, sliced on the diagonal
- 2 teaspoons thyme leaves
- 1 celery stalk, sliced on the diagonal
- 200 g (7 oz) sweet potato, sliced on the diagonal
- 1 cup dried Persian red lentils
- 5 cups vegetable or chicken stock
- 2 bay leaves
- 1 teaspoon sea salt
- ¼ teaspoon freshly ground black pepper
- 8 pitted black olives, sliced

Creamy green dahl

A delightfully easy dish to make, dahl is traditionally served with basmati rice. It's an age-old combination that provides a complete protein meal. I use split mung beans in this recipe, but split green peas will work just as well – just be sure to cook them in more water for a longer period to soften them.

Drain the mung beans and kombu and set aside until needed.

Heat the oil in a heavy-based saucepan over medium heat and add the mustard and cumin seeds. Once the seeds start to pop, add the garlic, ginger, chilli, onion and a pinch of sea salt and sauté for 2–3 minutes, or until softened.

Add the ground turmeric, cumin and coriander to the pan and sauté for 2 minutes, stirring well. Add the mung beans, kombu and 3 cups water. Bring to the boil, then reduce the heat to low and simmer for 25 minutes. Add the spinach, ½ teaspoon sea salt, lemon juice and coriander and cook for a further 5 minutes, or until the spinach has wilted.

Serve immediately with Steamed Millet (page 74), Steamed Quinoa (page 75) or steamed basmati rice.

Serves 4

1½ cups dried mung beans, soaked overnight in enough water to cover with a 3 cm (1¼ in) piece of kombu

1 tablespoon coconut oil

1 teaspoon black mustard seeds

1 teaspoon cumin seeds

1 garlic clove, crushed

2 cm (¾ in) knob of ginger, finely chopped

¼ teaspoon finely chopped green chilli

1 onion, diced

sea salt

1 teaspoon ground turmeric

1 teaspoon ground cumin

1 teaspoon ground coriander

100 g (3½ oz) baby spinach leaves, washed and roughly chopped

1 tablespoon lemon juice

2 tablespoons roughly chopped coriander (cilantro) leaves

Warm spiced chickpeas in orange tahini sauce

I often find myself craving this dish in winter. It's an adaptation of a meal I enjoy at my local Moroccan soup kitchen. Serve it up warm over some couscous or with toasted pita bread triangles. If you're in a hurry, use canned chickpeas (garbanzo beans) instead.

Drain the chickpeas and kombu and add to a heavy-based saucepan with 2 cups water. Bring to the boil, then reduce the heat to low and simmer for 30–45 minutes, or until the chickpeas soften. Remove from the heat and allow to cool in the cooking liquid.

To make the orange tahini sauce, place all the ingredients in a bowl and whisk together to combine. Set aside until needed.

Heat the oil in a deep frying pan over low heat. Add the onion and garlic with a pinch of sea salt and sauté for 3 minutes, or until softened. Add the ginger, ground turmeric, coriander, cumin and cayenne pepper and sauté for a further 2 minutes, stirring to combine.

Add the cauliflower with the stock or water, cover, and cook for 3 minutes, or until the cauliflower is tender. Add the chickpeas with 1 teaspoon sea salt and cook for a further 2 minutes, mixing well. Remove the pan from the heat and stir through the orange tahini sauce, then fold in the peas and herbs and serve.

Serves 4

1 cup dried chickpeas (garbanzo beans), soaked overnight in enough water to cover with a 3 cm (1¼ in) piece of kombu

1 tablespoon extra virgin olive oil

1 onion, diced

1 garlic clove, crushed

sea salt

2 cm (¾ in) knob of ginger, finely chopped

½ teaspoon ground turmeric

¼ teaspoon ground coriander

¼ teaspoon ground cumin

¼ teaspoon cayenne pepper (optional)

200 g (7 oz) cauliflower, cut into florets

3 tablespoons Vegetable Stock (page 39) or water

200 g (7 oz) fresh peas, blanched

1 tablespoon roughly chopped coriander (cilantro) leaves

1 tablespoon roughly chopped mint leaves

ORANGE TAHINI SAUCE

3 tablespoons hulled tahini

3 tablespoons orange juice

1 tablespoon finely grated orange zest

1 tablespoon shoyu

3 tablespoons plain yoghurt

1 tablespoon mirin

Broad bean, fennel and artichoke sauté

Broad beans, also known as fava beans, are truly Mediterranean, and are gorgeous in soups, salads and dips. This dish is an opportunity for the broad beans to shine amid some other spring offerings. If you like, serve warm over some toasted sourdough bread.

Heat 2 tablespoons oil in a frying pan over medium heat and sauté the garlic for 2 minutes, or until golden. Add the onion and sauté for a further 3 minutes, or until softened.

Layer the artichokes over the onion in the pan and add 3 tablespoons water. Cover and allow the artichokes to steam for 7 minutes, then add the broad beans and another 1–2 tablespoons water. Return the lid to the pan and steam for a further 5 minutes, or until the vegetables are nearly cooked through.

Add the fennel and parsley to the pan, season with the sea salt and freshly ground black pepper, then cover and cook for 2 minutes, or until all the liquid has evaporated. Fold through the preserved lemon and the remaining oil and serve warm.

Serves 4

2½ tablespoons extra virgin olive oil

2 garlic cloves, crushed

¼ onion, finely sliced

4 large fresh artichokes, trimmed and quartered

400 g (14 oz) shelled broad (fava) beans

½ fennel bulb, halved lengthwise, core removed, thinly sliced

2 tablespoons roughly chopped flat-leaf (Italian) parsley

1 teaspoon sea salt

¼ teaspoon freshly ground black pepper

1 tablespoon finely sliced preserved lemon

Lima beans
in velvety red sauce

This is my version of a sweet red sauce, which coats the cooked lima (butter) beans, and can be served by itself with brown rice or steamed quinoa. This rich and wonderful sauce also goes well with pasta.

Drain the beans and kombu and add to a saucepan with 2 cups water. Bring to the boil, then reduce the heat to low and simmer for 30–40 minutes, or until the beans are tender. Remove from the heat and allow to cool in the cooking liquid.

To make the red sauce, heat 1 tablespoon oil in a heavy-based saucepan over medium heat. Add the onion and garlic and sauté for 3–4 minutes, or until softened. Stir in the carrot, pumpkin, beetroot and celery. Pour in enough water to half-cover the vegetables, season lightly with sea salt and add the bay leaf. Cover the pan, bring to the boil, then reduce the heat to low and simmer for about 25 minutes, or until the vegetables are soft.

Remove the pan from the heat and allow to cool; discard the bay leaf. Pour the mixture into a food processor and process until smooth. Return the sauce to a clean pan and add the umeboshi paste and season with sea salt. Stir in the basil and the remaining oil.

Drain the cooked beans and add to the pan with the sauce, stirring to coat the beans and heat through. Serve warm over some Millet and Cauliflower Mash (page 74), Steamed Quinoa (page 75), Simple Polenta (page 71) or on top of your favourite pasta.

Serves 4

2 cups dried lima (butter) or cannellini beans, soaked overnight in enough water to cover with a 3 cm (1¼ in) piece of kombu

RED SAUCE

2 tablespoons extra virgin olive oil

1 onion, diced

1 garlic clove, crushed

½ carrot, cut into large chunks

200 g (7 oz) pumpkin, cut into 2 cm (¾ in) cubes

60 g (2 oz) fresh beetroot (beet), diced

2 celery stalks, diced

sea salt

1 bay leaf

1 teaspoon umeboshi paste or vinegar

2 tablespoons finely sliced basil leaves

Sweet and sour baked pinto beans

This is a truly warming, heartfelt dish to enjoy on cold winter nights. Cook it slowly it to create an amazing depth of flavour. If you like, substitute kidney or borlotti (cranberry) beans for the pinto beans. Serve with a dollop of Millet and Cauliflower Mash (page 74) or mop up with some chunky sourdough bread.

Drain the pinto beans and kombu and add to a heavy-based saucepan with the onion, carrot and 2 cups water. Bring to the boil, then reduce the heat to low and simmer for 10 minutes, skimming the surface to remove any scum. Cover and continue to simmer for 40 minutes, or until the beans are nearly soft.

Preheat the oven to 180°C (350°F/Gas Mark 4). Add the sea salt, vinegar, mustard and rice syrup to the pan and stir together to combine. Pour the mixture into a 2 litre (70 fl oz) casserole dish, cover, and bake in the oven for 20 minutes, or until the beans and vegetables are soft. Stir through the bonito flakes and herbs and serve over rice or baked polenta.

Serves 4

1 cup dried pinto beans, soaked overnight in enough water to cover with a 3 cm (1¼ in) piece of kombu

1 onion, diced

1 carrot, sliced on the diagonal

1 teaspoon sea salt

2 tablespoons brown rice vinegar

2 teaspoons grain mustard

2 tablespoons rice syrup

¼ cup bonito flakes (optional)

½ cup roughly chopped oregano or basil leaves

Gingered adzuki and pumpkin casserole

This soul-soothing casserole is the perfect accompaniment to a simple grain dish. Add lashings of freshly squeezed ginger juice to bring life and excitement to this dish. You can also treat this recipe as a sauce or even a dip. All you need do is cook it down until everything is overcooked, then whiz it all together. This is not the prettiest dish in the kitchen, but it tastes fantastic and will pick you up anytime you're feeling down.

1 cup dried adzuki beans, soaked overnight in enough water to cover with a 3 cm (1¼ in) piece of kombu

400 g (14 oz) pumpkin, cut into 2 cm (¾ in) chunks

½ onion, cut into 1 cm (½ in) wedges

1 tablespoon shoyu

1 tablespoon mirin

2 tablespoons ginger juice (see Note)

1 teaspoon sea salt

2 tablespoons finely sliced spring onion (scallion)

Drain the adzuki beans and kombu and add to a heavy-based saucepan with 2½ cups water. Bring to the boil over high heat and cook, uncovered, for 10 minutes. Reduce the heat to low, add the pumpkin and onion, cover and simmer for 30 minutes, or until beans are cooked.

Add the shoyu and simmer until all the liquid has been absorbed. Drizzle with the mirin and ginger juice, season with the sea salt and top with the spring onion to serve.

Serves 4

Note: Grate an 8 cm (3¼ in) knob of ginger, place in a muslin cloth (cheesecloth) and squeeze out the juice.

Seafood

Cooking with seafood can seem complicated – the fear of getting it wrong often stops people from buying some enticing fresh fish or prawns (shrimp) at the market. Memories of times tried and failed with seafood tend to stick in our mind.

As with anything though, the more often you cook with seafood, the easier the process becomes. The recipes in this chapter have been tried and tested many times by people who have attended my cooking classes over the years – so rest assured it is indeed possible to cook fish and seafood with ease.

Fish is a nutrient-packed food. It is a good quality source of protein and doesn't contain the high saturated fats found in other meats. Fish, especially oily fish such as salmon, is a terrific source of omega-3 fatty acids, which are known to help lower blood pressure, assist the heart and improve cardiovascular function. So, not only does it taste terrific, fish also leaves you feeling well.

Here are some simple steps to help you learn to swim (and cook) with the fishes:

Buy fresh fish from a local market. Start a relationship with a fishmonger you trust and be led by their expert recommendations.

Try to follow a sustainable fish policy. Buy fish that are from local waters. Wild sea or river fish is preferred over farmed fish every time. Your friendly fishmonger can help you explore this.

Buying whole fish is almost a guarantee of its freshness – yet many people find this prospect too scary to tackle. Once fish has been filleted it's much harder to assess its freshness. Some vendors claim snap-frozen fish as fresh fish, but for me any fish that has spent time in the freezer will definitely lose its joy when defrosting. Fresh fish shouldn't be slimy – it should be uniformly firm to the touch and smell like a fresh and salty sea breeze.

Store fish at or below 4°C (40°F), well sealed in an airtight container. Ideally store the fish over some ice.

Serve fish with a lemon or lime wedge, some freshly grated ginger or some freshly grated daikon on the side as they will all help make fish more digestible.

Combine fish with raw salads or steamed or boiled greens for an easily digestible meal. Avoid combing fish with starchy grains for a cleaner, more balanced meal.

Steamed rockling with basil vinaigrette

Although steaming seems a delicate method of cookery, you still need to be careful as where the fish sits can get mighty hot. Check your fish while it's hidden in the bamboo basket, as it can quickly overcook. This method of cooking fish is light, healthy and clean.

Line a bamboo steamer with baking paper or lightly oil a stainless steel steamer then place a single layer of fish inside. Sprinkle over a little sea salt. Place the steamer over a saucepan of boiling water, cover the steamer, and allow the fish to steam for about 7 minutes, or until firm to the touch – it should break away easily between your fingers.

Meanwhile, to prepare the basil vinaigrette, put the oil, vinegar, onion, tomato and sliced olives in a saucepan over low heat and cook for 5 minutes, or until the onion and tomato soften slightly. Stir through the lemon juice and basil.

To serve, carefully lift the fish fillets onto serving plates and spoon over some of the warm vinaigrette.

Serves 4

4 boneless, skinless rockling, ling or cod fillets (about 200 g/7 oz each)

sea salt

BASIL VINAIGRETTE

3 tablespoons extra virgin olive oil

3 tablespoons red wine vinegar

½ red (Spanish) onion, diced

1 tomato, diced

8 pitted black olives, sliced

3 tablespoons lemon juice

2 tablespoons finely sliced basil leaves

Crispy baked whitebait with lemon

Whitebait are a great source of calcium as you eat the entire fish, bones and all. Bake them until crunchy, add lots of parsley and eat quickly. Add some oil prior to cooking if you need it, or serve with some mayonnaise.

If using fresh, medium-sized sardines, have them gutted and remove the head. If using whitebait, keep whole, rinse and drain thoroughly. Pat the fish dry with paper towel.

Preheat the oven to 175°C (350°F/Gas Mark 4). Line a baking tray with baking paper. Place the flour, sea salt and freshly ground black pepper into a plastic bag with the fish and shake the bag well, making sure the fish are well coated.

Arrange the fish on the prepared tray and brush lightly on one side with the oil. Add the parsley and a generous pinch of sea salt and cook for 15–20 minutes, or until crisp and lightly browned – you will need to turn the fish during cooking so that they don't stick together.

Remove the fish from the oven and drizzle with lemon or lime juice. Serve hot with an extra lemon or lime wedge.

Serves 4

500 g (1 lb 2 oz) whitebait or sardines

½ cup rice flour

sea salt and freshly ground black pepper

1 tablespoon extra virgin olive oil

3 tablespoons roughly chopped flat-leaf (Italian) parsley

2 tablespoons lemon or lime juice

1 lemon or lime, cut into wedges

Lemon coconut fish

This delish fish recipe requires you to go to an Asian grocer to hunt for the marinade ingredients – that's the only difficult part! This marinade also works well in a Thai-style vegetable and tofu curry.

To make the marinade, put the onion, garlic, lemongrass, ginger, turmeric, galangal, chilli and coriander root in a food processor and process until smooth. Add the coconut cream and continue to blend until well incorporated.

Pour the marinade over the fish fillets in a bowl, adding the kaffir lime leaves. Cover with plastic wrap and refrigerate for 1 hour.

Add the fish and half the marinade to a frying pan over medium heat with the tomato and sea salt, and cook for 7 minutes, or until the fish flakes easily. Alternatively, cook the fish under a hot grill (broiler).

Serve with a generous squeeze of lemon juice and a scattering of basil and mint leaves.

Serves 4

½ onion, diced

1 garlic clove, crushed

2 tablespoons finely sliced lemongrass

2 cm (¾ in) knob of ginger, finely chopped

1 cm (½ in) knob of turmeric, finely chopped, or 1 teaspoon ground turmeric

2 cm (¾ in) knob of galangal, finely chopped

½ small red chilli, seeded and sliced

8 coriander (cilantro) roots, finely chopped

200 ml (7 fl oz) coconut cream

2 kaffir lime leaves

4 boneless blue grenadier (hoki/whiptail) fillets (about 200 g/7 oz each), or any other tender white fish fillets

1 tomato, cut into thin wedges

½ teaspoon sea salt

2 teaspoons lemon juice

2 tablespoons finely sliced Thai basil leaves

2 tablespoons roughly chopped mint

Baked salmon
with raw vegetable slaw

This is a dish with great contrast – a refreshing and crunchy raw salad served with baked salmon. The flavours and textures are reminiscent of summer eating. The salmon may also be served chilled if you like.

Preheat the oven to 170°C (340°F/Gas Mark 3). Line a baking tray with baking paper. Whisk together the shoyu, rice syrup and vinegar in a large bowl. Add the salmon to the bowl, turning to coat in the marinade, then cover and refrigerate for 10 minutes.

To make the slaw, put the carrot, celery, capsicum, and cabbage in a bowl. Add the lime juice and toss to combine. Refrigerate until needed.

Remove the salmon from the marinade and place the fillets, skin side down, on the prepared tray. Cook for 10 minutes, or until the fish just flakes when tested with a fork.

Stir the coriander and mint into the slaw mixture and spoon over the hot salmon.

Serves 4

Note: If you'd prefer to serve this dish chilled, allow the salmon to cool for 10 minutes at room temperature before covering and refrigerating. Serve crumbled with the raw slaw as a summer salad.

1 tablespoon shoyu

1 tablespoon rice syrup

1 tablespoon rice vinegar

4 boneless salmon fillets (about 185 g/6½ oz each), skin on, or any other oily fish fillets, such as tuna or ocean trout

SLAW

½ carrot, grated

1 celery stalk, cut into fine matchsticks

½ red capsicum (pepper), cut into fine matchsticks

200 g (7 oz) white cabbage, shredded

3 tablespoons lime juice

3 tablespoons chopped coriander (cilantro) leaves

2 tablespoons chopped mint leaves

Spiced fish fingers with lemon mayo

The Moroccan-inspired spice mix makes this fish dish deliciously exotic. I cut the fish into fingers so you get more spice to the bite. These can be eaten with your hands, so are great for a stand-up party. Or, for a fuller meal, serve with some crisp bitter greens.

To prepare the lemon mayo, drain the silken tofu in the fridge for 1–2 hours in a fine sieve over a bowl. This helps to remove excess liquid so that the mayonnaise doesn't become too watery. Place the tofu in a food processor with the other ingredients and process to make a smooth sauce. Cover and refrigerate until needed.

To prepare the spice mix, grind the ingredients separately either in a mortar with a pestle or a spice grinder to make a well blended powder. Store in an airtight container until needed.

Cut the fish fillets into thick, even-sized strips widthways to make fish fingers. Roll the fish in the spice mix to coat generously on both sides and season with sea salt.

Heat the oil in a frying pan over medium heat and cook the fish for 2–3 minutes on each side, depending on the thickness, or until the fish flakes when tested with a fork.

Serve the fish with some lemon mayo and lemon wedges on the side.

Serves 4

LEMON MAYO
300 g (10½ oz) silken tofu
2 tablespoons olive oil
1 teaspoon rice syrup
2 tablespoons lemon juice
1 tablespoon preserved lemon rind, finely chopped
¼ teaspoon sweet white miso

SPICE MIX
2 tablespoons sweet paprika
1 tablespoon freshly ground black pepper
1 tablespoon cumin seeds
1 tablespoon coriander seeds
1 teaspoon cardamom seeds
¼ teaspoon star anise

4 boneless, skinless flathead or whiting fillets (about 185 g/ 6½ oz each), or any other firm, white fish fillets
2 tablespoons extra virgin olive oil
sea salt
1 lemon, cut into wedges

Fish in the bag

This is my foolproof method of cooking fish. Make sure you buy a white-fleshed, boneless fillet of fish. These parcels can be made hours before guests arrive and refrigerated until they're ready to go into the oven. They are always impressive, although it can get a bit messy trying to elegantly slip the fish onto a plate. So, the best way is to serve it in its 'bag' on a plate and let your guests take on the challenge themselves.

Preheat the oven to 170°C (340°F/Gas Mark 3). Heat 2 tablespoons oil in a frying pan over medium heat and sauté the leek, carrot, capsicum, fennel and a pinch of sea salt for 3–4 minutes, or until the vegetables soften. Remove to a bowl and allow to cool.

Cut four 30 cm (12 in) square pieces of baking paper. Divide the vegetable mixture evenly between each square and place a fish fillet in the centre, on top of the vegetables.

Prepare a dressing by mixing together the remaining oil in a bowl with the wine and a little sea salt. Pour the dressing evenly over the vegetables and fish.

Arrange three lemon slices on top of each fish fillet and sprinkle over the combined mint and dill. Fold the edges of the paper over the fish to create a pouch and firmly seal each parcel. Place the parcels on a baking tray and cook for 10–15 minutes, or until the fish flakes easily when tested with a fork. Serve at the table in the parcels.

Serves 4

4 boneless, skinless barramundi fillets (about 200 g/7 oz each), or any other firm, white fish fillets

½ leek, white part only, cut into fine matchsticks

1 carrot, cut into fine matchsticks

1 red capsicum (pepper), cut into fine matchsticks

½ fennel bulb, finely sliced

140 ml (4¾ fl oz) extra virgin olive oil

3 tablespoons dry white wine

sea salt

1 lemon, finely sliced into rounds

1 small handful mint leaves

1 small handful chopped dill

Barbecued sweet-glazed seafood

This method of barbecuing seafood was inspired by street vendors in Japan and involves an easy, no-fuss, sweet-tasting glaze that is sure to please. If you prefer, substitute the prawns (shrimp) with any oily fish, such as tuna, salmon fillets or even medium-sized sardines. Serve with some freshly picked greens. If you're using wooden skewers remember to soak them in water for about 1 hour to prevent them burning during cooking.

Prepare the glaze by combining the shoyu, mirin, orange juice and palm sugar in a saucepan and bringing to the boil over high heat. Reduce the heat to low and simmer for 5 minutes, or until the sugar has dissolved. Remove from the heat and stir through the orange zest and ginger juice. Set aside until needed.

Preheat a barbecue hotplate or chargrill pan to medium–high. Thread a prawn, a piece of calamari and a scallop onto each skewer until all the seafood is used. Brush a little sesame oil onto the barbecue hotplate and place the skewers on top. With another brush, coat the fish with the marinade and continue coating as it absorbs. After 3 minutes, turn the seafood over and continue to brush with the marinade to thoroughly coat. Barbecue the seafood for another 3 minutes, or until the prawns are firm and the meat turns white. Serve straight from the barbecue, sprinkled with toasted sesame seeds, a pinch of coriander and a lime wedge.

Serves 4

Note: Grate a 1 cm (½ in) knob of ginger, place in a muslin cloth (cheesecloth) and squeeze out the juice.

8 metal or wooden skewers

8 large raw prawns (shrimp), shelled and deveined

8 rectangles of calamari/squid (about 20 g/¾ oz per piece)

8 scallops

GLAZE

2 tablespoons shoyu

2 tablespoons mirin

3 tablespoons orange juice

2 tablespoons grated palm sugar (jaggery)

1 tablespoon finely grated orange zest

1 teaspoon ginger juice (see Note)

1 tablespoon dark roasted sesame oil

1 tablespoon toasted sesame seeds (optional)

2 tablespoons roughly chopped coriander (cilantro) leaves

1 lime, cut into wedges

Seared tuna with sticky shiitake sauce

This robust piece of oily fish is matched with a vigorous style of cooking and served with a hearty sauce – it's all designed to feed a hungry person in need of some heavy-duty sustenance. Oily fish are fine left pink in the centre, although it may be best to ask your guests how they like theirs cooked before you do it your way.

To prepare the shiitake sauce, first drain the mushrooms, reserving the soaking liquid. Remove any woody stems and thinly slice the caps. Set aside until needed.

Heat the sesame oil in a deep frying pan over low heat and sauté the onion for 10 minutes, or until soft and translucent. Add the shiitake soaking liquid, the sliced mushrooms, mirin and shoyu and simmer for a further 10 minutes.

Increase the heat to high and bring the mixture to the boil. Add the kuzu mixture and stir continuously for 2 minutes, until it becomes thick and translucent. Remove the pan from the heat and add the spring onion and ginger juice. Keep warm.

Preheat a barbecue hotplate or chargrill pan to high. Brush the tuna steaks on both sides with sesame oil and sprinkle over some sea salt. Sear each side for 3–4 minutes, depending on the thickness of the fish. Serve with a good dousing of the shiitake sauce.

Serves 4

Note: Grate an 8 cm (3¼ in) knob of ginger, place in a muslin cloth (cheesecloth) and squeeze out the juice.

SHIITAKE SAUCE

10 dried shiitake mushrooms, soaked overnight in 1 cup water

1 tablespoon dark roasted sesame oil

2 onions, finely sliced

2 tablespoons mirin

2 tablespoons shoyu

1 cup water

3 teaspoons kuzu or arrowroot dissolved in 3 teaspoons cold water

2 tablespoons finely sliced spring onion (scallion)

2 tablespoons ginger juice (see Note)

4 boneless tuna fillets (about 185 g/6½ oz each), or any other oily fish, such as salmon or ocean trout

2 tablespoons dark roasted sesame oil

sea salt

Whiting covered in tahini on a roasted lemon bed

This is an exquisitely rich fish dish, which has a luscious mouthfeel. You could substitute the tahini sauce with macadamia or cashew butter for variation.

To make the tahini sauce, combine the tahini, lemon juice, shoyu, ginger juice and 2 tablespoons water in a bowl and whisk to create a smooth sauce. If it's too thick add a little extra water. Set aside until needed.

Preheat the oven to 170°C (340°F/Gas Mark 3). Grease a 2-litre (70 fl oz) baking dish with enough oil to coat. Arrange the lemon slices in the bottom of the dish and place the fish fillets in an even layer over the top. Sprinkle with a pinch of sea salt and drizzle lightly with oil. Bake for 7 minutes, then pour the tahini sauce over the fish and return to the oven for a further 7 minutes, or until the fish is cooked – the sauce will brown and begin to bubble.

Remove from the oven and allow to cool for a few minutes as the tahini sauce sets. Spoon out and serve warm with the baked lemon slices and coriander and mint leaves. If you like, sprinkle with Nut and Seed Condiment (page 210). This fish is also excellent served at room temperature or cold.

Serves 4

Note: Grate a 1 cm (½ in) knob of ginger, place in a muslin cloth (cheesecloth) and squeeze out the juice.

TAHINI SAUCE
3 tablespoons hulled tahini
½ cup lemon juice
1 tablespoon shoyu
2 tablespoons water
1 teaspoon ginger juice (see Note)

4 boneless whiting fillets (about 200 g/7 oz each), or any other firm, white fish fillets
extra virgin olive oil
2 lemons, sliced into rounds
sea salt
1 tablespoon finely chopped coriander (cilantro) leaves
1 tablespoon finely chopped mint leaves

Chicken

Of all the meat available to us, I tend to gravitate towards chicken. I search out organic, free-range birds that have pecked and scratched all day long and snoozed underneath the shade of a tree, enjoying the good life.

Meat is a highly developed protein food and of these, I find that poultry is the lightest and easiest to digest. I have days where I crave a small piece of chicken, only to find that it makes me feel great the day after. Chicken is warming and offers strengthening possibilities – and we all know about the healing powers of the almighty chicken soup. I choose chicken when I need a real pick-me-up – after some heavy physical work, or if I'm feeling ill or run down.

Here are my chicken tips:

The most important consideration when cooking with chicken is to choose an organic or biodynamic and free-range bird. Buy a whole bird and have your butcher separate the thighs and breasts. The breasts contain the least amount of fat so require less cooking, otherwise they quickly become dry. The thighs are filled with muscle tissue and sinew, so require a longer, slower cooking time to break down and become tender.

To cook the breasts, remove and discard the skin, cut the meat into strips and cook quickly over high heat in a stir-fry. Other methods that work well with chicken breast include grilling (broiling) and pan-frying. To cook chicken thighs, use longer methods of cookery, such as casseroling or stewing.

I find that marinating chicken not only helps to tenderise the meat but it also adds complexity of flavour and aids digestion. We want a good flavoured bird but also one that we can stomach easily. Marinades may include citrus, vinegar, yoghurt or a range of fermented foods. I take a lot of inspiration from the many Asian cuisines where poultry is often a small part of the final dish and is found among vegetables, spices and stock.

I serve chicken with a variety of simply cooked greens or a side of bitter salad greens, which leaves you with a happy tummy.

Whole chicken and mushrooms braised in soy

The rich mushroom and soy combination makes for a full-flavoured dish. The chicken is softened in the marinade then slowly braised so that the flavours penetrate deeply. Serve with some wok-fried bok choy (pak choy).

Rinse the chicken and pat dry with paper towel. Combine all of the marinade ingredients in a bowl, then massage into the skin of the chicken halves and set aside in the refrigerator for 30 minutes.

Heat the sesame oil in a wok or large heavy-based frying pan over high heat and sauté the ginger and garlic for 2 minutes, or until starting to brown. Add the leek, button mushrooms and five-spice powder and sauté for 2 minutes, stirring to combine. Drain the marinade from the chicken and add the chicken halves to the wok with 1 cup water.

Bring the liquid to the boil, then reduce the heat to low and simmer for 20 minutes. Add the shiitake and oyster mushrooms to the wok, cover, and braise for a further 10 minutes, or until the thighs are cooked. Increase the heat to high and bring the mixture to the boil. Add the kuzu mixture and stir continuously for 2 minutes, until the liquid is thickened and clear. Reduce the heat to low.

Remove the chicken from the pan and cut each breast in half and remove the wings, then cut the thighs in half at the joint. Return the chicken pieces to the wok and stir to combine. Serve the chicken and mushrooms topped with the fresh enoki mushrooms and coriander leaves.

Serves 4

Note: Grate a 4 cm (1½ in) knob of ginger, place in a muslin cloth (cheesecloth) and squeeze out the juice.

MARINADE
⅓ cup mirin
⅓ cup soy sauce
1 tablespoon ginger juice (see Note)

1 kg (2 lb 4 oz) whole chicken, halved lengthwise
2 tablespoons dark roasted sesame oil
1 tablespoon finely sliced ginger
3 garlic cloves, crushed
1 leek, white part only, cut into rounds
8 button mushrooms, quartered
¼ teaspoon five-spice powder
100 g (3½ oz) fresh shiitake mushrooms, quartered
150 g (5½ oz) oyster mushrooms
2 teaspoons kuzu or arrowroot dissolved in 2 teaspoons cold water
100 g (3½ oz) enoki mushrooms
3 tablespoons roughly chopped coriander (cilantro) leaves

Baked chicken with sage and lemon

Here is a no-fuss tangy chicken dish for that lazy Sunday lunch. Get organised and marinate the pieces a day in advance, then serve with either a plate of roast vegetables, green beans or a fresh garden salad. Leftovers also taste great served cold the following day.

Cut the chicken in half through the centre. Remove the thighs from the carcass and cut through the joint creating two pieces from both thighs. Take each breast, with bones intact, cut in half through the bone and slice away the wing. This gives you 10 pieces. Wash the chicken and dry thoroughly with paper towel.

Make the marinade by whisking together the mustard, lemon juice, lemon zest, oil and salt in a bowl. Rub the marinade all over the chicken pieces, then sprinkle on the sage leaves and refrigerate for 1–2 hours.

Preheat the oven to 175°C (350°F/Gas Mark 4). Place the chicken pieces in a baking dish and bake for about 30 minutes, then turn each piece over and bake for a further 30 minutes, or until cooked through. Meanwhile, chargrill the lemon halves, cut side down, for about 5 minutes, or until dark and caramelised. Serve the chicken with the sage leaves, chargrilled lemon and a salad.

Serves 4

1.2 kg (2 lb 10 oz) whole chicken

1 tablespoon hot or dijon mustard

½ cup lemon juice

finely grated zest of 1 lemon

⅓ cup extra virgin olive oil

1 teaspoon sea salt

10 sage leaves

2 lemons, cut in half

Stir-fried sesame chicken on green tea noodles

This is a great tasting, salty, sesame flavoured chicken, which is served with noodles to soak up the delicious sauce. Try marinating your bird the night before as it will tenderise and flavour a little more. You may vary the noodles you use, depending on how hungry you are. Green tea noodles are often made with buckwheat flour so are generally hearty, but sometimes you may feel like a softer, easy-going rice noodle.

Place all the marinade ingredients in a bowl and whisk to combine. Toss the chicken pieces through the marinade to coat and refrigerate for at least 1 hour.

Drain the chicken pieces, reserving the marinade. Heat the sesame oil in a wok or large heavy-based frying pan over high heat and sauté the chicken for 5 minutes, or until golden. Add the marinade as the chicken begins to stick to the pan and turn to coat.

Add the kuzu mixture to the wok and stir through the sauce, turning to coat the chicken in the shiny glaze. Add the sesame seeds, carrot, capsicum and cabbage to the wok and continue to stir-fry for a further 2 minutes, or until the vegetables soften slightly.

Meanwhile, cook the green tea noodles using the 'shock' method (page 146).

Serve the hot chicken and vegetables over the cooked green tea noodles and top with coriander.

Serves 4

MARINADE

1 tablespoon shoyu

1 tablespoon mirin

1 teaspoon sake

2 teaspoons brown rice vinegar

½ teaspoon dark roasted sesame oil

1 cm (½ in) knob of ginger, finely chopped

1 garlic clove, crushed

1 skinless, boneless chicken breast fillet, cut into long strips

1 tablespoon dark roasted sesame oil

2 teaspoons kuzu or arrowroot dissolved in 2 teaspoons cold water

1 tablespoon roasted sesame seeds

½ carrot, cut into matchsticks

½ red capsicum (pepper), cut into matchsticks

100 g (3½ oz) red cabbage, finely shredded

125 g (4½ oz) green tea noodles

2 tablespoons roughly chopped coriander (cilantro) leaves

Sweet and sour chicken swimming with greens

This recipe is a great way of getting greens into your meal. Practise thickening liquids with kuzu or arrowroot as the result makes for a beautiful visual glaze.

Prepare the sweet and sour sauce by combining the ingredients in a bowl. Set aside until needed.

Heat the sesame oil in a wok or heavy-based frying pan over medium heat and sauté the garlic and ginger for 1 minute. Add the chicken and cook for 3 minutes, stirring to brown the chicken all over. Add the stock and bring to the boil. Add the beans and broccoli, reduce the heat to low, cover, and simmer for 2 minutes. Add the baby corn, sugar snap peas and water chestnuts and cook for a further minute, or until the peas soften slightly.

Pour the sauce into the simmering wok, stirring constantly for 1 minute as the sauce thickens. Remove the wok from the heat, add the spring onions and serve the chicken and vegetables over some steamed rice or cooked noodles.

Serves 4

SWEET AND SOUR SAUCE

3 tablespoons brown rice vinegar

1 tablespoon mirin

2 tablespoons shoyu

2 tablespoons barley malt

2 tablespoons kuzu or arrowroot dissolved in 2 tablespoons cold water

1 tablespoon dark roasted sesame oil

1 garlic clove, crushed

2 cm (¾ in) knob of ginger, finely chopped

2 large boneless, skinless chicken breast fillets, cut into 2 cm (¾ in) cubes

1 cup Vegetable Stock (page 39) or chicken stock

150 g (5½ oz) green beans, trimmed and halved

150 g (5½ oz) broccoli florets

4 baby corn, halved

100 g (3½ oz) sugar snap peas or snow peas (mangetout), trimmed

230 g (8 oz) canned water chestnuts, drained

2 tablespoons finely sliced spring onion (scallion)

Baked chicken in crisp vine leaves

The recipe comes from a friend, who cooks it when catering for hundreds of people at a time. It's easy to prepare in advance, cooks easily and presents well. If you're not in the mood to whip up the mayo, then just buy a good homemade version and add some finely chopped preserved lemon. Search out preserved vine leaves from a European delicatessen or greengrocer. You will need to soak the leaves in cold water for an hour to remove any excess saltiness.

Prepare the lemon mayo by placing all the ingredients in a food processor or blender and processing for 2 minutes to make a purée, then cover and refrigerate until needed.

To make the spice mix, combine all the ingredients in a bowl and mix thoroughly.

Rinse the chicken breasts and pat dry with paper towel. Roll each breast in the spice mix to coat, dusting off any excess. Place on a large plate. Take two vine leaves per breast, patting them dry. Wrap the vine leaves across each breast and seal the leaves with a little oil – try to keep the seal on the underside of each breast. Use a pastry brush to brush oil over the vine leaves, then refrigerate for at least 30 minutes.

Preheat the oven to 180°C (350°F/Gas Mark 4). Transfer the chicken to a lightly oiled baking tray, making sure you leave plenty of space between the breasts, then sprinkle with the oregano. Bake for 15 minutes, or until cooked through.

Slice each breast into pieces and serve hot with the lemon mayo. This chicken dish tastes great with some freshly picked tomatoes, cucumber chunks, feta, dried oregano and a drizzle of extra virgin olive oil and lemon juice.

Serves 4

LEMON MAYO
300 g (10½ oz) silken tofu

1 tablespoon extra virgin olive oil

2 tablespoons finely chopped preserved lemon

1 tablespoon lemon juice

1 teaspoon rice syrup

½ teaspoon dijon mustard

pinch of ground turmeric

pinch of salt

pinch of freshly ground black pepper

SPICE MIX
2 teaspoons ground cumin

2 teaspoons ground coriander

2 teaspoons ground ginger

1 teaspoon ground chilli

½ teaspoon ground cinnamon

½ teaspoon ground turmeric

¼ teaspoon ground cloves

1 teaspoon freshly ground black pepper

½ teaspoon sea salt

2 teaspoons finely grated orange zest

4 skinless, boneless chicken breast fillets

8 large vine leaves, soaked in water for 1 hour

2 tablespoons extra virgin olive oil

1 tablespoon dried oregano

Lime and fig chicken

This delicious chicken dish has wonderfully contrasting sweet and sour flavours from the lime juice and fig jam. Substitute with plums or apricots if figs are not in season.

Use a sharp knife to butterfly each chicken breast – slice open the thick part of the breast to make a larger, flatter, thinner breast. You may gently pound with a meat mallet to make it even all over if you wish.

Heat 1 tablespoon oil in a frying pan over medium heat. Working in two batches, add the chicken breasts and cook on each side for 3 minutes, or until lightly golden. Season, then remove to a plate and keep warm. Repeat with the remaining oil and chicken. Cut each breast into four long batons.

Add the lime juice, fig jam and fresh figs to the pan over medium heat, stirring well. Simmer for 3 minutes, then gently return all the chicken to the pan. Coat with the sauce and serve warm topped with the mint and coriander.

Serves 4

4 skinless, boneless chicken breast fillets

2 tablespoons extra virgin olive oil

sea salt and freshly ground black pepper

⅓ cup lime juice

⅓ cup fig jam

4 ripe figs, quartered

1 tablespoon roughly chopped mint leaves

1 tablespoon roughly chopped coriander (cilantro) leaves

Crisp chicken with raisin and olive vinaigrette

This dish was inspired by one of my many mistakes. It was meant to be crumbed chicken breasts, until I realised I didn't have any breadcrumbs but still needed to create an impressive meal in a hurry. The dressing is also a collection of some pantry staples that came to the party.

Cut each breast into 3 diagonal pieces of roughly equal thickness to create 12 pieces in total. Put the flour in one bowl, whisk the egg yolks with 2 tablespoons water in another bowl, and add the cornmeal to a third bowl. Roll each piece of chicken in the flour, shaking off any excess, then dip into the egg mixture before rolling in the cornmeal to coat. Set aside on a tray.

Heat half the oil in a frying pan over medium heat, then add half the chicken pieces with a touch of sea salt and freshly ground black pepper. Cook for 3–4 minutes on each side, or until golden and firm to the touch. Remove from the pan and repeat with the remaining oil and chicken.

Meanwhile, prepare the vinaigrette by combining the ingredients in a saucepan over low heat. Simmer for 3 minutes, or until the onion and tomato soften slightly.

Remove the cooked chicken from the pan and divide between serving plates, then pour the vinaigrette over the top. Sprinkle with the pine nuts and parsley and serve.

Serves 4

4 skinless, boneless chicken breast fillets

⅓ cup unbleached white flour

2 egg yolks

½ cup fine polenta (cornmeal)

⅓ cup olive oil

sea salt and freshly ground black pepper

⅓ cup toasted pine nuts

2 tablespoons flat-leaf (Italian) parsley

VINAIGRETTE

3 tablespoons extra virgin olive oil

3 tablespoons balsamic vinegar

¼ red (Spanish) onion, diced

½ tomato, seeds removed and diced

3 tablespoons raisins

4 pitted green olives, halved

Creamy coconut and basil chicken

This is a gently spiced chicken for those days when the temperature cools down. The addition of coconut cream makes this dish especially luscious. If you'd like the sauce to become thicker and even creamier in texture, dissolve two teaspoons of kuzu or cornflour (cornstarch) in two teaspoons of cold water and add it to the simmering chicken. For a complete meal, serve this dish over noodles or rice.

To make the spice mix, combine the ingredients in a bowl and mix together.

Rinse the chicken and pat dry with paper towel. Toss through the dry spice mixture to coat, then set aside in the fridge for 30 minutes.

Heat 1 tablespoon oil in a frying pan over medium heat and sauté half the chicken pieces for 4 minutes, stirring, or until golden. Transfer the chicken to a bowl and set aside. Repeat with 1 tablespoon oil and the remaining chicken.

Heat the remaining oil in a separate frying pan over medium heat. Add the onion and cook for 3 minutes, or until softened. Add the garlic, ginger and chilli and cook for a further 3 minutes. Return the chicken pieces to the pan with the coconut cream mixture, lemon juice and zest and the kaffir lime leaves. Simmer for 10 minutes, or until the chicken is cooked through.

Serve warm with the Thai basil leaves and garlic chives sprinkled over the top and a squeeze of lime juice.

Serves 4

SPICE MIX

½ teaspoon ground cumin

½ teaspoon ground coriander

¼ teaspoon ground cloves

¼ teaspoon ground cinnamon

¼ teaspoon ground cardamom

½ teaspoon freshly ground black pepper

¼ teaspoon ground turmeric

½ teaspoon sea salt

500 g (1 lb 2 oz) boneless, skinless chicken thigh fillets, cut into 2 cm (¾ in) pieces

3 tablespoons coconut oil

1 red (Spanish) onion, diced

3 garlic cloves, crushed

1 cm (½ in) knob of ginger, finely chopped

1 small red chilli, finely sliced

270 ml (9½ fl oz) coconut cream, mixed with 3 tablespoons water

freshly squeezed juice and finely grated zest of 1 lemon

2 kaffir lime leaves

1 handful Thai basil leaves

1 handful garlic chives

1 lime, cut in half

Soy

At one time, the thought of adding soy to your diet would have had others thinking you were about to join a commune. Thankfully, times have changed.

The two soy products that make it on my 'eat occasionally' list are tofu and tempeh. Both are derivatives of the sacred soy bean. In their dry form, soy beans are indigestible, regardless of how long you soak or cook them. Hence, the Chinese stumbled upon tofu, which is pressed soy bean curds.

Tofu is a nutritious, lean source of protein that may also contain good quantities of calcium, depending on how it's made. When purchasing any soy products search out certified organic products that are free from genetic modification.

Tofu is available in various grades of firmness, which are useful for creating different dishes. Firm tofu acts a little like a sponge – by itself it has a neutral taste but readily absorbs the other flavours of a dish. Firm tofu is easily marinated, baked, braised or stir-fried. It is so adaptable that it can suit Italian, Mexican, Thai, Japanese or Chinese dishes. One of the most flavoursome ways of preparing tofu is to grill (broil) or shallow-fry it. The oil seals the tofu, so it develops a chewy textured skin that helps to retain its firmness.

Silken tofu is simply soy milk that has been thickened. This makes it ideal for dips, creams and silky desserts.

Tofu is available vacuum-packed or fresh in tubs at health food stores, organic grocers and supermarkets. Once opened, it must be immersed in water in an airtight container and refrigerated. Change the water daily and use the tofu within a week. If you've got some leftover tofu, you can also freeze it. Once defrosted it will return with a chewy, porous texture that lends itself to making great satisfying steaks for grilling (broiling).

Tofu is a concentrated protein with a strong cooling effect in the body, therefore it should be eaten in moderation. Prepare tofu with warming spices such as ginger or mustard to balance its cooling nature.

My favourite soy food is tempeh, which is a staple of Indonesia. Unlike tofu, tempeh uses the whole soy bean and through its culturing process, which is similar to making aged cheeses, produces a high-quality, digestible protein food that is also rich in carbohydrates and fibre.

You can find tempeh in the refrigerated section at the supermarket, organic grocers, health food stores and select Asian grocers. Tempeh should remain refrigerated and be consumed within a week of opening, or frozen for later use. Keep it sealed at all times – there's no need to immerse it in water.

Tempeh must be thoroughly cooked before eating it. You can prepare it many ways: slice it thinly or thickly, or cut it into small cubes and fry it in different oils for a variety of flavours. Eat as you would chips (French fries) or add to sandwiches, stir-fries, salads or noodles. Tempeh is meaty in texture and flavour. So for those in need of a good source of excellent quality protein, sink your teeth into tempeh.

Steamed tofu nori rolls with ginger dipping sauce

These nori rolls are a great party recipe – but don't just pass them around, let your guests get involved in making them too. These are to be eaten instantly, so dig in as soon as they're cooked!

To prepare the dipping sauce, combine the ingredients in a bowl and stir in 3 tablespoons water. Set aside until ready to serve.

Heat the sesame oil in a frying pan over medium heat and sauté the onion, garlic and ginger for 3 minutes, or until softened. Add the carrot and mushroom and sauté for a further 3 minutes. Crumble the tofu into the pan and season with the shoyu and mirin. Continue to stir for 2 minutes, or until the liquid has been absorbed. Remove the pan from the heat and stir through the parsley and coriander.

To assemble the rolls, lay a nori sheet shiny side down on a bamboo rolling mat, making sure the longest side is directly in front of you on the bench. Press 4 heaped tablespoons of the tofu mixture into the centre of the roll, and flatten out, leaving a 2 cm strip on the two long sides. Use a wet pastry brush to lightly brush the border furthest from you as this will help the roll stick together. Starting at the end closest to you, roll the nori sheet to make a neat log and firmly encase the filling. Repeat with the remaining nori sheets and filling to make six nori rolls in total.

Working in batches, place two nori rolls at a time into a bamboo steamer over a saucepan of boiling water and steam for 7 minutes. They'll be a little delicate when done, so remove them gently and allow to cool slightly before slicing and dipping.

Serves 4

DIPPING SAUCE

½ cup shoyu

2 teaspoons finely grated ginger

1 tablespoon finely sliced spring onion (scallion)

1 teaspoon dark roasted sesame oil

½ onion, finely chopped

1 garlic clove, crushed

2 cm (¾ in) knob of ginger, finely chopped

¼ carrot, grated

5 button mushrooms, sliced thinly

250 g (9 oz) firm tofu, crumbled

1 tablespoon shoyu

1 tablespoon mirin

1 tablespoon roughly chopped flat-leaf (Italian) parsley leaves

1 tablespoon roughly chopped coriander (cilantro) leaves

6 toasted nori sheets

Tofu and shiitake hotpot

This warming casserole can become even more wholesome by adding some fresh rice noodles or cooked buckwheat (soba) noodles. It has a traditional Japanese flavour with a fresh, spring-green lightness.

Pat the tofu dry with paper towel to remove any excess moisture. Heat 1 tablespoon sesame oil in a frying pan over medium heat and fry the tofu for 3–5 minutes, or until golden. Transfer to a bowl of warm water to remove any excess oil, then drain, press out any excess water and set aside.

Drain the shiitake mushrooms, reserving the soaking liquid. Trim the stems and slice the caps. Slice the kombu into strips.

Heat 1 teaspoon sesame oil in a heavy-based saucepan over medium heat and sauté the onion and ginger for 3 minutes, or until softened. Add the shiitake, kombu, carrot, daikon and 2 cups of the shiitake soaking water to the pan. Increase the heat to high, bring to the boil, then reduce the heat to medium–low, cover, and simmer for 10 minutes, or until the carrots are almost tender.

Add the tofu, bok choy and enoki mushrooms and simmer for 3 minutes, then stir in the mirin and shoyu and cook for a further 2 minutes. Remove the pan from the heat, and divide the hotpot between bowls.

Serves 4

250 g (9 oz) firm tofu, cut into 1 cm (½ in) cubes

1 tablespoon and 1 teaspoon dark roasted sesame oil

5 dried shiitake mushrooms, soaked in 2 cups water

3 cm (1¼ in) length kombu, soaked in ½ cup water

½ onion, finely sliced

2 cm (¾ in) knob of ginger, finely sliced

1 carrot, sliced diagonally

½ daikon, sliced diagonally

100 g (3½ oz) baby bok choy (pak choy) or choy sum (Chinese flowering cabbage), chopped

50 g (1¾ oz) enoki mushrooms

1 tablespoon mirin

1 tablespoon shoyu

Sweet and sour tempeh, corn and pumpkin nishime

This is an easy one-pot dish that hails from the Japanese style of braising called 'nishime'. You simply layer vegetables in a pan and braise them in liquid to slowly develop a satisfying sweetness. You can alter the ingredients, but make sure the onion goes in first before adding the remaining vegetables – from firmest to flimsiest. No need to stir as they become intimate when left alone. Serve on rice, with noodles or as a casserole.

Heat the sesame oil in a heavy-based frying pan over medium heat and sauté the tempeh for 3–5 minutes, turning until crisp and golden. Remove, cut into triangles and set aside to drain on paper towel.

Lay the onions in the base of a clean frying pan, followed by the pumpkin and corn kernels. Add enough water to come halfway up the vegetables. Season with sea salt, cover, and simmer for 7 minutes over low heat, or until the pumpkin is almost cooked.

Put the mirin, shoyu, lemon juice, ginger juice and kuzu mixture in a bowl and stir to dissolve the kuzu.

Add the cooked tempeh to the pan with the vegetables, then quickly stir in the dressing so that it coats the other ingredients. Remove from the heat and serve.

Serves 4

Note: Grate a 1 cm (½ in) knob of ginger, place in a muslin cloth (cheesecloth) and squeeze out the juice.

2 tablespoons dark roasted sesame oil

150 g (5½ oz) tempeh, cut into 3 mm (⅛ in) strips

1 onion, cut into thick wedges

300 g (10½ oz) pumpkin, cut into 2 cm (¾ in) cubes

1 corn cob, kernels removed

sea salt

2 tablespoons mirin

1 tablespoon shoyu

2 teaspoons lemon juice

1 teaspoon ginger juice (see Note)

2 teaspoons kuzu or arrowroot dissolved in 2 teaspoons cold water

Tofu and
coconut cream curry

This Thai-inspired curry will work well with tofu and vegetables, fish or chicken. Adjust the chilli according to your preference. It freezes well and can be stored in the refrigerator for up to three days.

Pat the tofu dry with paper towel to remove any excess moisture. Heat the sesame oil in a frying pan over medium heat and fry the tofu for 3–5 minutes, or until golden. Transfer to a bowl of warm water to remove any excess oil, then drain, press out any excess water and set aside.

To make the curry paste, place all of the ingredients in a food processor and process to make a smooth purée. Heat a heavy-based saucepan over medium heat and sauté the curry paste for 5 minutes, stirring continuously, until fragrant. If it becomes too dry, add a little more water.

Add the sweet potato and pumpkin with 1 cup water and simmer for 7 minutes. Add the coconut cream, tomato wedges and season with sea salt. Cook for a further 5 minutes, or until the sweet potato and pumpkin are soft. Stir through the tofu, Thai basil and lemon juice, top with the green beans and serve over steamed jasmine rice or noodles.

Serves 4

200 g (7 oz) firm tofu, cut into 2 cm (¾ in) cubes

1 tablespoon dark roasted sesame oil

200 g (7 oz) sweet potato, cut into 2 cm (¾ in) cubes

200 g (7 oz) pumpkin, cut into 2 cm (¾ in) cubes

400 ml (14 fl oz) coconut cream

2 tomatoes, cut into wedges

sea salt

2 tablespoons roughly chopped Thai basil leaves

2 teaspoons lemon juice

150 g (5½ oz) green beans, trimmed and blanched

CURRY PASTE

½ onion, diced

1 tablespoon chopped ginger

1 teaspoon chopped turmeric or ½ teaspoon ground turmeric

1 tablespoon chopped galangal

1 tablespoon finely chopped lemongrass

1 garlic clove, crushed

½ teaspoon chilli, sliced

8 coriander (cilantro) roots, finely chopped

2 kaffir lime leaves

Creamy tempeh and carrot casserole

This hearty tempeh casserole is destined to warm your insides on a cold night. I make large amounts of this casserole and serve it over some spiral pasta or, if I can't wait for the pasta to cook, I simply eat as is with a side of blanched greens.

Heat half the oil in a frying pan over medium heat and sauté the tempeh for 3–5 minutes, or until crisp and golden. Remove, cut into 1 cm (½ in) cubes and set aside to drain on paper towel.

Heat the remaining oil in a heavy-based saucepan over low heat. Add the onion and garlic and cook for 3 minutes, or until softened. Add the carrot and 3 tablespoons stock, cover, and simmer for 5 minutes, or until the liquid has almost evaporated.

Add the remaining stock to the pan, bring to the boil, cover, and simmer for 8–10 minutes, or until the carrots are tender. Increase the heat to high and bring the casserole to the boil. Add the kuzu mixture and stir vigorously for 1 minute. Once the sauce has thickened, reduce the heat to low, add the peas and cooked tempeh.

Mix together the miso, mustard and shoyu in a bowl and spoon 2 tablespoons of the casserole liquid into it, stirring to dissolve the miso and mustard. Pour this back into the casserole and simmer for 2 minutes.

Remove from the heat, add the parsley and serve over Steamed Brown Rice (page 79), Steamed Millet (page 74) or your favourite noodles.

Serves 4

2 tablespoons olive oil

300 g (10½ oz) tempeh, cut into 1 cm (½ in) cubes

1 onion, diced

1 garlic clove, crushed

2 carrots, sliced diagonally

2 cups Vegetable Stock (page 39)

1 tablespoon kuzu or arrowroot dissolved in 1 tablespoon cold water

150 g (5½ oz) freshly shelled peas

3 teaspoons white miso

1 teaspoon dijon mustard

2 teaspoons shoyu

1 tablespoon roughly chopped flat-leaf (Italian) parsley

Tempeh and asparagus with roasted capsicum and olive dip

The combination of blanched greens with fried tempeh makes for an interesting spring or summer dish. For a little Moroccan magic, add a teaspoon of smoked paprika to the dip.

To make the dip, preheat the oven to 200°C (400°F/Gas Mark 6). Roast the capsicum for 5–10 minutes, or until the skin is black and blistered. Transfer to a plastic bag and allow to sweat for 30 minutes before removing and discarding the skin and seeds. Chop the flesh and place in a food processor with the remaining ingredients and process to make a smooth purée. Set aside until ready to serve.

Heat the sesame oil in a heavy-based frying pan over medium heat and sauté the tempeh for 3–5 minutes, or until crisp and golden. Add the shoyu and mirin, stir to coat the tempeh then quickly remove and set aside.

Blanch the green beans, broccoli and asparagus separately in boiling water until *al dente*, then drain and place in a serving bowl.

Add the avocado slices, oil and lemon juice to the bowl and toss to combine. Season with sea salt. Arrange the tempeh strips on plates and pile the greens on top. Serve at room temperature with the dip on the side and the lemon halves.

Serves 4

ROASTED CAPSICUM AND
  BLACK OLIVE DIP
1 red capsicum (pepper)
10 pitted black olives, chopped
1 garlic clove, crushed
2 tablespoons roughly chopped
  basil leaves
¼ cup ground almonds or
  breadcrumbs
1 small chilli, finely chopped
  (optional)
⅓ cup extra virgin olive oil
2 tablespoons red wine vinegar
sea salt and freshly ground
  black pepper

1 tablespoon dark roasted
  sesame oil
150 g (5½ oz) tempeh, cut into
  3 mm (⅛ in) strips
1 tablespoon shoyu
1 tablespoon mirin
200 g (7 oz) green beans,
  trimmed
200 g (7 oz) broccoli florets
200 g (7 oz) asparagus spears,
  trimmed and halved
½ avocado, cut into thin slices
1 tablespoon extra virgin
  olive oil
1 teaspoon lemon juice
sea salt
2 lemons, halved

Chilli and orange grilled tofu with Asian greens

This is an easy to prepare, digest and cook recipe – perfect for those newcomers to tofu. I like to serve this with some brown rice, millet or quinoa. Don't feel tied down to using Asian greens as Italian-style bitter greens will work just as well, fried in a little garlic.

To make the marinade, put the ingredients in a bowl and stir well to combine.

Cut the tofu into rectangles about 5 mm (¼ in) thick. Cut each rectangle diagonally to make 2 triangles. Place the tofu triangles in a deep dish and pour the marinade over the top. Marinate in the fridge for at least 1 hour.

Heat a barbecue grill or chargrill plate to high and brush with a little sesame oil. Cook the tofu for at least 3 minutes on each side, or until sealed and brown. Remove from the heat and keep warm.

Meanwhile, add 1 teaspoon sesame oil to a wok over medium–high heat and sauté the ginger and leek for 3–4 minutes, or until the leek wilts. Add the snake beans and 2 tablespoons water, cover and steam for 3 minutes. Add the bok choy and choy sum and sauté for 3–4 minutes, or until the greens wilt but remain firm and crisp. Add the sesame seeds and coriander and stir to combine. Serve topped with the grilled tofu.

Serves 4

MARINADE

1 teaspoon finely grated ginger

1 garlic clove, crushed

1 teaspoon finely grated orange zest

¼ teaspoon chilli, finely chopped (optional)

1 tablespoon shoyu

1 tablespoon mirin

¼ teaspoon dark roasted sesame oil

500 g (1 lb 2 oz) firm tofu

dark roasted sesame oil

2 cm (¾ in) knob of ginger, cut into thin strips

1 leek, white part only, sliced diagonally

100 g (3½ oz) snake (yard-long) beans, cut into 3 cm (1¼ in) lengths

2 bunches bok choy (pak choy), cut into large pieces

2 bunches choy sum (Chinese flowering cabbage), cut into large pieces

1 teaspoon roasted sesame seeds

2 teaspoons roughly chopped coriander (cilantro)

Grilled marinated tempeh on sweet and sour cabbage

The ever-versatile tempeh is perfect partnered with cabbage. I often eat this dish between two fat slices of toasted sourdough bread, but it's also excellent served with steamed millet or buckwheat.

To make the marinade, put the ingredients in a bowl and stir well to combine. Add the tempeh, toss to coat, and marinate in the fridge for at least 2 hours.

If you are using wooden skewers, soak them in water for about 1 hour to prevent them from burning during cooking. Preheat a grill (broiler) or barbecue grill plate to high.

To prepare the sweet and sour cabbage, heat the oil in a heavy-based frying pan over medium heat and sauté the onion for 3 minutes, or until softened. Add the cabbage and a pinch of sea salt and sauté for 3–4 minutes, or until the cabbage wilts. Pour in the orange juice, balsamic vinegar and rice syrup and stir to combine. Cover, reduce the heat to low and simmer for 7 minutes, or until the cabbage softens. Just before serving, stir through the pine nuts, orange zest and parsley.

Meanwhile, thread the marinated tempeh cubes onto the skewers. Place the skewers onto an oiled tray or brush the barbecue plate with oil. Broil or barbecue for 7–8 minutes, until browned lightly on all sides and the centre is warm. Serve over the warm sweet and sour cabbage.

Serves 4

MARINADE

1 teaspoon ground cumin

1 garlic clove, crushed

1 cm (½ in) knob of ginger, finely chopped

2 tablespoons white miso

1 tablespoon mirin

1 teaspoon finely grated lemon zest

300 g (10½ oz) tempeh, cut into 2 cm (¾ in) cubes

metal or wooden skewers

1 tablespoon extra virgin olive oil

½ red (Spanish) onion, finely sliced

250 g (9 oz) red cabbage, finely shredded

sea salt

3 tablespoons orange juice

3 tablespoons balsamic vinegar

2 tablespoons rice syrup

50 g (1¾ oz) roasted pine nuts

1 teaspoon finely grated orange zest

1 tablespoon roughly chopped flat-leaf (Italian) parsley leaves

Baked lemon and sesame tofu steaks

This recipe is a lunchbox favourite of mine. It tastes great hot, but is even better served cold in a sandwich. I often serve these tofu steaks with garlicky toasted bread and layer it with pickled cucumber, slices of tomato, red (Spanish) onion slivers and ripe avocado.

Preheat the oven to 170°C (340°F/Gas Mark 3). Cut the tofu into eight rectangular slices, about 1 cm (½ in) thick. Pat the tofu dry with paper towel to remove any excess moisture.

Place the remaining ingredients in a bowl and whisk to a pourable consistency, adding a little water if it's too thick.

Lightly oil a shallow baking dish and place the tofu slices in the base. Pour over the lemon and sesame mixture, making sure the tofu is completely coated in the sauce. Bake for 10 minutes, or until the sauce has firmed up and is golden. Carefully remove the steaks and eat immediately, or refrigerate for tomorrow's lunch.

Makes 8 steaks

500 g (1 lb 2 oz) firm tofu
½ cup hulled tahini
1 tablespoon wholegrain mustard
3 tablespoons lemon juice
finely grated zest of 1 lemon
2 tablespoons finely chopped flat-leaf (Italian) parsley leaves
1 tablespoon brown rice syrup
2 tablespoons brown rice vinegar
1 tablespoon shoyu
3 tablespoons roasted sesame seeds

Noodles & pasta

Noodles and pasta are enjoyed by many people and cultures across the globe. The Chinese simmer their clear cellophane (bean thread) noodles in delicate broths, the Japanese slurp their saucy buckwheat (soba) noodles with abandon and the Italians gulp down copious amounts of spaghetti.

When combined with a bean sauce or a soy food, your noodle or pasta dish moves towards being a complete and satisfying meal.

Noodles and pasta come in many dazzling shapes and sizes and are made from a variety of different flours. Some are bought dry and others fresh. Pasta is often made from wheat flour, with added water and salt. Japanese-style noodles, by contrast, are made with a combination of flours, such as buckwheat or rice, and sometimes wheat flour. Chinese-style dried noodles are often made from rice starch or mung beans, while fresh noodles are often made with rice flour.

I prepare noodles and pasta two ways: by traditional method and by 'shock' method.

The traditional method is used for most pasta recipes that call for cooking *al dente*. To prepare pasta using this method, first bring a large saucepan of boiling water to a strong, rolling boil, remove the lid and add the pasta, stirring continuously so that it doesn't stick together. Add a teaspoon of salt to enhance the flavour. To see if it's done, take one strand and cut it. It should be firm and cooked right through, but not mushy.

I use the shock method for Japanese-style noodles, such as buckwheat (soba) and udon (wholewheat). These noodles are hardier, more wholesome, very flavoursome and can withstand extreme cooking conditions. To prepare noodles with this method, bring a large saucepan of water to the boil, drop in the noodles, stir them and quickly add a cup of cold water to 'shock' them. Repeat this method of 'shocking' up to three times and then check the noodle for doneness. The noodle is ready when cooked through but still firm. Refresh the noodles under cold running water if they are to be used later and add a teaspoon of sesame oil so they don't stick together.

Over the years I've had fun experimenting with noodles and pasta and the following recipes are some of my favourites.

Braised bean thread hot pot

This dish has oodles of slippery and satisfying noodles combined with a tangy orange and ginger sauce. Rice vermicelli also works well with this recipe.

Soak the noodles in a bowl of hot water for 20 minutes. Drain and set aside. Trim the stems from the shiitake mushrooms and finely slice the caps.

Heat the sesame oil in a frying pan or wok over medium heat and sauté the garlic, ginger, onion, carrot, cabbage and shiitake with a sprinkling of sea salt for 3–5 minutes, or until the vegetables soften. Transfer to a plate and set aside.

Add the marinade ingredients to a heavy-based saucepan over medium heat with ½ cup water. Simmer for about 5 minutes, or until the liquid reduces by half. Add the drained noodles and stir for about 3 minutes, until they absorb the marinade.

Add the stir-fried vegetable mixture to the pan and toss gently to combine. Cover and continue to simmer for 2 minutes. Add the kuzu mixture to the pan and stir to thicken the noodle mixture. Once the noodles are glazed, top with coriander leaves and a sprinkling of roasted sesame seeds.

Serves 4

175 g (6 oz) dried cellophane (bean thread) noodles

5 dried shiitake mushrooms, soaked overnight in ½ cup water

1 tablespoon dark roasted sesame oil

2 garlic cloves, finely sliced

2 cm (¾ in) knob of ginger, cut into fine matchsticks

½ onion, finely sliced

½ carrot, finely sliced

150 g (5½ oz) Chinese cabbage, chopped

sea salt

1 teaspoon kuzu or arrowroot dissolved in 1 teaspoon cold water

2 teaspoons coriander (cilantro) leaves

1 tablespoon roasted sesame seeds

MARINADE
½ cup orange juice

2 tablespoons shoyu

2 tablespoons mirin

1 teaspoon finely grated orange zest

1 teaspoon dark roasted sesame oil

Fried gingered rice noodles with prawns

This is a terrific meal that you can cook in minutes. If you don't even have the time to add the prawns (shrimp), then forget them and the dish will be ready even sooner. I use my well-worn wok and sometimes can't help but eat directly from it – when no one's around of course! If you like, substitute the prawns with 200 g (7 oz) of stir-fried tofu or tempeh and it will still taste delicious.

Heat half the sesame oil in a frying pan or wok over medium heat. Add the prawns and fry for 7 minutes, or until pink and firm. Set aside on paper towel.

Heat the remaining sesame oil in a frying pan or wok over medium heat and sauté the garlic and ginger for 1 minute. Add the onion, a pinch of sea salt and enough water to cover the base of the pan. Cover and cook for about 5 minutes, until the onion is soft. Add the carrot and mushroom and simmer for 3–5 minutes, or until tender. Add the corn and sugar snap peas, then add the noodles and prawns. Cover and simmer over low heat for 3 minutes – you may need to add a little water to prevent the vegetables from sticking.

Stir through the shoyu, mirin and ginger juice. Serve hot with cashews and coriander on top.

Serves 4

Note: Grate a 4 cm (1½ in) knob of ginger, place in a muslin cloth (cheesecloth) and squeeze out the juice.

2 teaspoons dark roasted sesame oil

12 raw prawns (shrimp), shelled and deveined, tails left intact

1 garlic clove, crushed

2 cm (¾ in) knob of ginger, cut into fine matchsticks

½ onion, finely sliced

sea salt

1 carrot, cut into fine matchsticks

5 button mushrooms, sliced

5 baby corn, halved

100 g (3½ oz) sugar snap peas or snow peas (mangetout), trimmed

200 g (7 oz) fresh flat rice noodles

2 tablespoons shoyu

3 tablespoons mirin

1 tablespoon ginger juice (see Note)

⅓ cup roasted cashews

1 tablespoon roughly chopped coriander (cilantro)

Chilled green tea noodles

This is a summertime lifesaver for those days when you're hungry but don't really want to cook. I use the hardier Japanese-style noodles because they can handle the acidic marinade and still taste great the following day.

Prepare the noodles using the 'shock' method (see page 146). Drain and rinse under cold running water, then drain again and set aside.

Bring a saucepan of water to the boil and blanch the carrots and snow peas, in separate batches, for about 2 minutes each, or until tender but still firm. Refresh the vegetables immediately under cold running water, then drain again. Slice the snow peas in half lengthways.

To make the dressing, whisk the ingredients in a bowl then pour over the cooked noodles. Add the carrot and snow pea with the onion and cucumber and toss to combine.

Allow the noodles to marinate in the dressing for at least 30 minutes in the fridge, then serve with the mint on top.

Serves 4

Note: Grate an 8 cm (3¼ in) knob of ginger, place in a muslin cloth (cheesecloth) and squeeze out the juice.

125 g (4½ oz) green tea noodles

½ carrot, cut into fine matchsticks

100 g (3½ oz) snow peas (mangetout), trimmed

¼ red (Spanish) onion, finely sliced

½ cucumber, finely sliced

1 small handful mint leaves

DRESSING

½ cup orange juice

1 tablespoon finely grated orange zest

2 tablespoons ginger juice (see Note)

1 teaspoon mirin

1 teaspoon brown rice vinegar

½ teaspoon shoyu

1 teaspoon dark roasted sesame oil

Udon noodles with wasabi and greens

This is another feel-good summer meal that can be served chilled when the weather heats up. To serve this dish warm, simply add the heated sauce and top with the raw ingredients as soon as the noodles are cooked. Toasted seeds are fantastic sprinkled over this dish.

Prepare the noodles using the 'shock' method (see page 146). Drain and rinse under cold running water, then drain again and set aside.

Bring a saucepan of water to the boil and blanch the spinach and rocket, in separate batches, for 1–2 minutes each, or until just wilted. Remove and refresh the vegetables immediately under cold running water, then drain again.

To make the sauce, place the ingredients in a saucepan over medium heat with 1/3 cup water. Stir for 3 minutes, then remove from the heat and set aside. Whisk the sauce to attain a smooth consistency – if it appears a little thick, add a little extra water to thin it out.

Toss the drained noodles with the blanched greens, cucumber and radicchio. Serve on plates and top with the sauce and spring onion. Serve warm or chilled.

Serves 4

125 g (4½ oz) udon noodles

150 g (5½ oz) baby spinach leaves

150 g (5½ oz) rocket (arugula) leaves

1 cucumber, finely sliced

1 small head of radicchio (Italian chicory)

3 tablespoons finely sliced spring onion (scallion)

SAUCE

2 garlic cloves, crushed

½ cup hulled tahini

1 tablespoon shoyu or umeboshi paste

1 tablespoon brown rice or apple cider vinegar

3 tablespoons lemon juice

1 teaspoon wasabi powder

½ teaspoon finely grated lemon zest

Spaghetti with broad bean pesto

This version of pesto, enriched with silken tofu and white miso, is well worth trying. Feel free to use broccoli, asparagus or fresh peas instead of the broad (fava) beans. If you're in the mood to make more changes, then go ahead and use mint or coriander (cilantro) instead of the basil.

Bring a saucepan of water to the boil, drop in the broad beans and cook for 5 minutes, or until tender but still firm. Refresh immediately under cold running water, then drain again. Remove the outer skins and discard.

Put the broad beans, garlic and pine nuts in a food processor and pulse until the mixture resembles breadcrumbs. Add the basil, oil, tofu, miso, half the lemon zest and the freshly ground black pepper and process to make smooth purée.

Meanwhile, cook the pasta in a saucepan of boiling salted water for 7 minutes, or until *al dente*. Drain the spaghetti and toss with the pesto sauce, making sure it is evenly coated. Serve in bowls with the remaining lemon zest sprinkled on top.

Serves 4

250 g (9 oz) shelled broad (fava) beans
1 garlic clove, crushed
3 tablespoons roasted pine nuts
2 large handfuls chopped basil
3 tablespoons extra virgin olive oil
300 g (10½ oz) silken tofu
2 teaspoons white miso
finely grated zest of 1 lemon
¼ teaspoon freshly ground black pepper
200 g (7 oz) spelt spaghetti

Lemon and lime linguini

This is a happy Italian noodle dish with some Asian inspiration. It's a bit like wearing your favourite summer outfit: it's easy, colourful and feels good.

Bring a large saucepan of water to the boil, drop in the fresh peas and cook for 3 minutes, or until tender. Refresh immediately under cold running water, then drain again.

Put the peas in a food processor with the lemon juice, lime juice, mirin and miso and pulse to make a smooth purée. Set aside until needed.

Cook the pasta in a saucepan of boiling salted water for 8–9 minutes, or until *al dente*. Drain and set aside.

Heat the oil in a large frying pan over medium heat. Add the pasta and lemon zest and toss until warmed through. Fold in the pea purée, coating the pasta completely. Serve immediately with the dill sprinkled on top.

Serves 4

400 g (14 oz) freshly shelled peas
100 ml (3½ fl oz) lemon juice
3 tablespoons lime juice
1 tablespoon mirin
2 tablespoons white miso
250 g (9 oz) wholemeal linguine
3 tablespoons extra virgin olive oil
2 teaspoons finely grated lemon zest
1 tablespoon chopped dill

Macaroni and prawns in warm olive and basil vinaigrette

This dish can be served warm but is also excellent served chilled as a salad. If you feel inclined, go ahead and substitute 200 g (7 oz) of cooked chickpeas (garbanzo beans) for the prawns (shrimp), but make sure that you cook them well or cheat and throw in half a can of organic chickpeas instead! Try to search out good-quality, handmade Italian macaroni from your local delicatessen.

Cook the macaroni in a large saucepan of boiling salted water for 8–9 minutes, or until *al dente*.

Meanwhile, heat the oil in a frying pan over medium heat and sauté the rosemary and garlic for 1 minute. Add the prawns and cook for 3 minutes, then add the onion with a pinch of sea salt and sauté for a further 3 minutes. Once the prawns are cooked and have changed colour, add the tomato and olives. Remove the pan from the heat and add the vinegar, and a pinch each of sea salt and freshly ground black pepper. Keep the sauce warm while you drain the macaroni.

Toss the macaroni thoroughly into the sauce to coat evenly. Add the basil leaves and serve.

Serves 4

400 g (14 oz) macaroni

3 tablespoons extra virgin olive oil

1 teaspoon rosemary leaves, finely chopped

1 garlic clove, crushed

200 g (7 oz) green prawns (shrimp), shelled and deveined

¼ red (Spanish) onion, diced

sea salt

½ tomato, diced

8 pitted green olives, sliced

2 tablespoons red wine vinegar

freshly ground black pepper

2 tablespoons torn purple basil leaves

Pizzoccheri with almond tofu and creamy mushroom sauce

Pizzoccheri is a flat ribbon pasta made from buckwheat flour that hails from the Italian Alps. This recipe is perfect for cold wintery days when all you want to do is curl up with a bowl full of creamy pasta. *Buon appetito*!

Cut the tofu into rectangles about 5 mm (¼ in) thick. Pat the tofu dry with paper towel to remove any excess moisture.

Heat 1 tablespoon oil in a frying pan over medium heat and fry the tofu for 3 minutes on each side, or until golden. Transfer to a bowl of warm water to remove any excess oil, then drain and squeeze out any water. Thinly slice the tofu on the diagonal to make fine strips and set aside.

Heat 1 tablespoon olive oil in a heavy-based saucepan over medium heat and sauté the garlic for 1 minute. Add the onion with a pinch of sea salt and sauté for 3 minutes, or until softened. Add the remaining oil with the mushrooms and sauté for 3 minutes. Add the ground almonds, soy milk and bouillion powder and simmer for 5 minutes, or until the mushrooms are cooked and the sauce has thickened.

Put the miso in a bowl and add 2 tablespoons of the warm sauce liquid, stirring well to dissolve the miso. Add back to the pan and continue to simmer for 3–4 minutes, then add the tofu slices and tarragon. Keep warm.

Cook the pasta in a saucepan of salted boiling water for 8–9 minutes, or until *al dente*. Drain and serve with the warm sauce and some freshly ground black pepper.

Serves 4

250 g (9 oz) firm tofu

3 tablespoons extra virgin olive oil

1 garlic clove, crushed

1 onion, diced

sea salt

250 g (9 oz) mushrooms, finely sliced

75 g (2¾ oz) ground almonds

1½ cups soy or almond milk

1 teaspoon vegetable bouillion (stock) powder (or 1 stock cube)

1 tablespoon white miso

2 tablespoons roughly chopped tarragon leaves

200 g (7 oz) pizzoccheri

freshly ground black pepper

Penne with pumpkin and walnut crema

Here's my version of a creamy vegetable sauce – without the cream. The sauce is sweet and nutty all in one mouthful. I often use this sauce as a filling for bakes or lasagne. You can also fold the penne into the sauce and bake it in the oven to make *pasta al forno.*

Preheat the oven to 175°C (350°F/Gas Mark 4). Place the pumpkin, onion and garlic in a baking tray. Drizzle with 3 tablespoons oil and sprinkle with some sea salt. Bake for about 45 minutes, or until the pumpkin is soft. Allow to cool, then remove the skin from the pumpkin and garlic.

Place the pumpkin, onion and garlic in a food processor with the orange juice and zest, miso, half the walnuts and the remaining oil. Process to make a smooth purée. Add more orange juice for a thinner sauce. Season to taste.

Cook the pasta in a saucepan of salted boiling water for about 6 minutes, or until almost *al dente*. Add the broccoli florets to the boiling water with the penne and blanch for 2–3 minutes, or until tender. Drain the penne and broccoli and toss together with the pumpkin sauce.

Serve the penne with basil, olives and the remaining chopped walnuts scattered on top.

Serves 4

400 g (14 oz) pumpkin, chopped into large chunks

½ onion, sliced into wedges

2 garlic cloves, unpeeled

⅓ cup extra virgin olive oil

sea salt

2 tablespoons orange juice

1 teaspoon finely grated orange zest

1 tablespoon white miso

100 g (3½ oz) walnuts, roasted and ground

freshly ground black pepper

300 g (10½ oz) penne rigate (penne with ridges)

180 g (6¼ oz) broccoli florets

2 tablespoons finely sliced basil leaves

8 pitted green olives, sliced

Greens

Greens

It's not often that we get complimented on a dish of greens at the table. But why shouldn't the greens shine? Many people tend to over- or under-cook their greens and leave them undressed and therefore un-exciting to the palette. We wouldn't think of serving a plain boiled chicken or fish without a sauce, marinade or spice, so why would we approach greens this way?

Greens are the planet's way of delivering one of the most nutrient-dense foods available. These foods, especially dark leafy varieties, are loaded with fibre, chlorophyll, calcium and vitamins A and C. Greens are an essential ingredient in a healthy diet.

When choosing greens, generally the smaller the leaf the milder the flavour – darker and larger leaves tend to have a stronger flavour. Different greens appear in every season and require different methods of preparation and flavouring.

I organise my greens into three groups: Asian greens, which include bok choy (pak choy), choy sum (Chinese flowering cabbage) and mustard greens – some are sweet and tender and others hardier and bitter; Italian greens, such as rocket (arugula), chicory and dandelion, most of which are hardy and have a degree of bitterness; and finally, firm greens, such as broccoli, asparagus, brussels sprouts, peas and green beans.

To prepare leafy greens, first remove any woody or hard stems as they never soften and their strong flavour can ruin a dish.

I use three methods of cooking greens: blanching, steaming and sautéing.

Blanching is a wet style of cooking and is suitable for firm and dry vegetables and greens such as broccoli, asparagus, green beans, peas and brussels sprouts.

To blanch greens, drop the vegetables into a small amount of boiling water in a saucepan.

The water should remain boiling throughout the cooking. Blanching is fast and helps retain crispness, nutrients and great looking greens.

Even when you remove a vegetable from the blanching pot it continues to cook. So, plunge it into cold water for a minute to stop the cooking process then drain. Keep tasting your greens as they cook and drain when *al dente* – slightly crisp on the inside and soft on the outside. As different vegetables have different cooking times, start by adding the firmest vegetable first, such as brussels sprouts, then something like green beans or broccoli and lastly peas and asparagus. Cooking times will also be influenced by the size of the vegetable and its freshness.

Steaming will create a dryer effect on your greens than blanching and is suitable for watery vegetables, such as zucchini (courgettes), spinach, squash and silverbeet (Swiss chard).

The steaming method is an intense way of cooking greens. It's faster than blanching and produces firmer vegetables. As steaming is a fast process, your greens may overcook quickly. Check the texture to ascertain whether they're ready or not.

Sautéing is a fast and furious way to cook your greens. The idea is to get a wok or frying pan hot, but not smoking. Add oil, garlic, ginger or chilli – or all three – then drop in the greens and stir continuously. Taste as you go and the idea is to retain a bright colour and sweet taste with minimal cooking.

The following recipes are some of my favourite greens matched with individual dressings and condiments.

Warm broad beans and friends in pear and orange dressing

This hearty dish of greens with a creamy citrus dressing is perfect served with Baked Chicken with Sage and Lemon (page 119) or Crispy Baked Whitebait (page 103).

Put the tahini in a large bowl. Gradually add the orange juice and whisk until the mixture becomes smooth. Add the pear, vinegar, shoyu, ginger and orange zest and continue whisking so it is a pourable consistency. If the dressing is too thick, add a little water to thin it. Set aside.

Bring a saucepan of water to the boil and blanch the broad beans, sugar snap peas and broccoli, in separate batches, for 3–5 minutes each, or until tender but still firm. Refresh the vegetables immediately under cold running water, then drain again.

Transfer the greens to a plate, top with the dressing and sprinkle over the coriander. Serve warm.

Serves 4

PEAR AND ORANGE DRESSING

3 tablespoons hulled tahini

3 tablespoons orange juice

⅓ cup finely grated pear

1 teaspoon brown rice vinegar

1 tablespoon shoyu

4 cm (1½ in) knob of ginger, finely grated

2 teaspoons finely grated orange zest

200 g (7 oz) shelled broad (fava) beans

200 g (7 oz) sugar snap peas or snow peas (mangetout), trimmed

200 g (7 oz) broccoli florets

1 tablespoon coriander (cilantro) leaves

Braised cabbage and carrots with roasted walnuts

This is a gorgeous looking vegetable dish, which is great served as an accompaniment to a rich meal. It has a sweet and sour flavour with a satisfying crunch – and tastes even more delicious the next day.

Heat half the oil in a heavy-based saucepan over medium heat and sauté the onion with a pinch of sea salt for 3 minutes, or until softened. Add the carrot and half the orange juice and simmer for 3 minutes.

Add the cabbage with the remaining orange juice, cover and cook for 5 minutes, or until the vegetables start to wilt.

Stir in the miso, rice syrup, rice vinegar and remaining oil and cook for 1 minute. Remove from the heat and stir in the dill and walnuts. Serve warm or allow to sit for 30 minutes, as the flavour improves, and then serve at room temperature.

Serves 4

2 tablespoons extra virgin olive oil

½ red (Spanish) onion, finely sliced

sea salt

1 carrot, cut into fine matchsticks

1 cup orange juice

200 g (7 oz) white cabbage, shredded

200 g (7 oz) red cabbage, shredded

1 tablespoon white miso

1 tablespoon brown rice syrup

2 tablespoons brown rice vinegar

1 teaspoon roughly chopped dill

30 g (1 oz) walnuts, roasted and chopped

Green beans rolling in toasted sesame seeds

This side dish can also be served cold as a salad. The dressing also works perfectly with blanched broccoli, asparagus or any tasty cooked greens. Try adding some torn mint and lime or lemon zest for a springtime feel.

Dry-fry the sesame seeds in a frying pan over low heat for 5–7 minutes, or until toasted and fragrant – they will begin to pop when ready. Transfer the sesame seeds to a mortar with a pestle or a spice grinder and pound or grind them until roughly crushed.

Combine the miso, rice syrup, vinegar and 2–3 tablespoons water in a saucepan over low heat and cook for 3 minutes, or until well combined and heated through. Add the ground sesame seeds, remove from the heat and set aside.

Bring a saucepan of water to the boil and blanch the beans for 4 minutes, or until tender but still crunchy. Refresh immediately under cold running water, then drain again.

Toss the beans with the sesame dressing and serve warm as a side dish, or allow to cool to room temperature and eat later as a salad.

Serves 4

50 g (1¾ oz) sesame seeds

2 tablespoons white miso

1 tablespoon brown rice syrup

1 tablespoon brown rice vinegar

500 g (1 lb 2 oz) green beans, trimmed

Wok–fried greens in lime and coconut

This is a delicious and quick Asian greens side dish with a little bite that goes well with seared tuna or tofu steaks.

To make the sauce, whisk the ingredients in a bowl to combine. Set aside.

Heat the sesame oil in a wok or heavy-based frying pan over high heat and sauté the garlic for 1 minute. Add the ginger and chilli and fry for a further minute before adding the cashews. Stir-fry for 2 minutes, or until the nuts brown.

Add the spring onion and Asian greens and stir-fry for 2–3 minutes, or until the leaves start to wilt. Increase the heat and stir in the sauce for 1 minute to coat the vegetables. Serve hot.

Serves 4

LIME AND COCONUT SAUCE

1 teaspoon shoyu

2 tablespoons lime juice

3 tablespoons coconut cream

1 teaspoon dark roasted sesame oil

1 garlic clove, finely sliced

1 slice ginger, cut into fine matchsticks

1 teaspoon chilli, seeds removed and cut into fine strips

30 g (1 oz) raw cashews

3 spring onions (scallions), finely sliced

3 bunches Asian greens (bok choy/pak choy or choy sum/ Chinese flowering cabbage), chopped

Warm asparagus with garlic tofu sauce

This is a feel-good sauce that reminds me of mayonnaise without the high fat content. Try adding a teaspoon of finely chopped preserved lemon or some roasted red capsicum (pepper) for added excitement.

Preheat the oven to 175°C (350°F/Gas Mark 4). Roast the garlic on a tray for 10 minutes, or until soft. Allow to cool, then peel the skin.

Place the garlic in a food processor with the remaining sauce ingredients and season with sea salt and freshly ground black pepper. Process to make a smooth purée. Transfer the sauce to a saucepan over low heat and keep warm until needed.

Bring a saucepan of water to the boil and blanch the asparagus for 3 minutes, or until tender but still firm. Refresh immediately under cold running water, then drain again.

Arrange the asparagus on a serving plate and spoon over the creamy sauce to serve.

Serves 4

GARLIC TOFU SAUCE

4 garlic cloves, unpeeled

150 g (5½ oz) silken tofu

1 tablespoon extra virgin olive oil

3 tablespoons champagne vinegar

1 tablespoon white miso

1 tablespoon dijon mustard

¼ teaspoon ground turmeric

finely grated zest of 1 lemon

sea salt and freshly ground black pepper

500 g (1 lb 2 oz) asparagus, trimmed

Baby beets and beet greens in horseradish salsa

Adding a little red colour to your day is always uplifting. If you're unable to find fresh horseradish, search for a good-quality horseradish in the jar.

Remove the green leaves from the beetroots and soak them in water. Scrub the beetroots and place in a saucepan. Cover with water, add a pinch of sea salt and bring to the boil over high heat. Reduce the heat to medium and simmer for 20 minutes, or until the beetroots are tender when pierced with a knife. Drain in a colander and allow to cool. Carefully remove the skins under cold running water and cut the beetroots into quarters. Set aside.

Wash the beet greens well, remove any hard stems and blanch in a saucepan of boiling water for 3–4 minutes, or until tender. Refresh immediately under cold running water, then drain again and set aside.

Put the yoghurt in a food processor with the horseradish, lemon juice, orange zest, oil, cumin, ¼ teaspoon sea salt and a pinch of freshly ground black pepper. Process to make a smooth purée.

Put the beetroots and greens in a bowl and toss through the yoghurt dressing to coat. Serve warm, topped with the coriander leaves.

Serves 4

500 g (1 lb 2 oz) baby beetroots (beets), with leaves intact

sea salt

250 g (9 oz) plain yoghurt

4 cm (1½ in) knob of horseradish, finely chopped, or 1 tablespoon horseradish paste

freshly squeezed juice of 1 lemon

finely grated zest of 1 orange

1 tablespoon extra virgin olive oil

1 teaspoon ground cumin

freshly ground black pepper

1 tablespoon coriander (cilantro) leaves

Zucchini, okra and roasted hazelnut braise

This is a quick and easy layered braise, made exciting with fresh spring herbs, sour lemon and crunchy hazelnuts. It's the perfect way to add extra greens to a meal.

Heat 1 tablespoon oil in a frying pan over medium heat and add the onion and garlic, then layer on the zucchini and okra. Sprinkle on the cumin, salt and stock or water. Bring to the boil, cover and simmer for 10 minutes, or until the vegetables have softened.

Drizzle the remaining oil into the pan with the lemon juice, then fold through the coriander, mint and hazelnuts. Season with freshly ground black pepper and serve warm.

Serves 4

2 tablespoons extra virgin olive oil

1 onion, finely sliced

1 garlic clove, finely sliced

2 zucchini (courgettes), cut into 5 cm (2 in) batons

200 g (7 oz) okra, halved lengthways

1 teaspoon ground cumin

½ teaspoon sea salt

½ cup Vegetable Stock (page 39) or water

3 tablespoons lemon juice

1 tablespoon finely chopped coriander (cilantro) leaves

1 tablespoon finely chopped mint leaves

2 tablespoons chopped roasted hazelnuts

freshly ground black pepper

Bitter greens in warm balsamic

This is my way of turning those winter bitter greens into a warming side dish. For those with a vegetable garden, try planting your own, such as the Asian mustard greens or the Italian leafy rapini (broccoli rabé). Or, if you like, choose some year-round self-seeding dandelion leaves or rocket (arugula) to go wild in your vegie patch.

Bring a saucepan of water to the boil and blanch the greens for about 3 minutes, or until wilted. Drain, squeeze out any excess water, and set aside.

Heat the oil in a frying pan over medium–low heat and sauté the onion and garlic with a pinch of sea salt for 10 minutes, or until the onion caramelises.

Add the blanched greens to the pan with the lemon juice and cook for 3 minutes, or until the liquid has evaporated. Stir in the balsamic vinegar, ¼ teaspoon sea salt and the freshly ground black pepper and remove from the heat. Stir through the lemon zest and serve warm.

Serves 4

200 g (7 oz) dandelion greens, chopped

200 g (7 oz) rapini (broccoli rabé), chopped

200 g (7 oz) beetroot (beet) leaves, chopped

200 g (7 oz) mustard greens, chopped

1 tablespoon extra virgin olive oil

1 red (Spanish) onion, finely sliced

1 garlic clove, crushed

sea salt

2 tablespoons lemon juice

2 tablespoons balsamic vinegar

¼ teaspoon freshly ground black pepper

1 teaspoon finely grated lemon zest

Brussels sprouts
with lemon miso dressing

This is my favourite brussels sprout recipe. Cutting them in half quickens the time it takes to get the dish on the table and cooking them right through creates extra sweetness.

To make the dressing whisk together the miso and mustard in a bowl. Slowly whisk in the oil and once emulsified, add the lemon juice and continue to whisk until completely incorporated. Stir in the parsley, rice syrup and enough freshly ground black pepper to taste. Set aside.

Bring a saucepan of water to the boil and blanch the brussels spouts for about 10 minutes, or until cooked – they taste better when fully cooked. Drain well.

Toss the brussels sprouts with the dressing so they absorb all the flavours. Serve warm or allow to sit for 30 minutes to soak up the dressing and then serve at room temperature.

Serves 4

LEMON MISO DRESSING

2 tablespoons white miso

2 teaspoons wholegrain mustard

3 tablespoons extra virgin olive oil

3 tablespoons lemon juice

2 tablespoons finely chopped flat-leaf (Italian) parsley

2 teaspoons brown rice syrup

freshly ground black pepper

500 g (1 lb 2 oz) brussels sprouts, trimmed and halved

Desserts

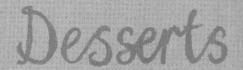

When I was a child, desserts were a very special comfort food – and since then, nothing much has changed!

The opportunity to bake and eat a natural wholefood dessert is always nourishing to me and I believe such foods have a place within a well-balanced, healthful diet.

Wholefood desserts are sadly viewed as tasteless and heavy affairs, so many people are put off from giving them a try. However, eating natural sweets does not mean depriving yourself of all things decadent and delicious.

You will find the following recipes satisfying and flavoursome without all the fat, dairy and refined sugars usually found in desserts and cakes. Of course, they'll never be as light and airy as the others, yet they'll taste divine with a definite feel good factor that will have you wanting more.

Creating desserts with natural wholefoods takes a little more time and thought as natural ingredients will react differently in the mix every time. You need to be prepared to experiment and ad lib where necessary.

Following are some suggestions for a successful journey with my favourite wholefood desserts:

Of the many varieties of flour, I tend to stock unbleached white or wholemeal spelt flour, which is my everyday flour used to create light desserts and partner it with coconut flour, almond meal or variations depending on the theme.

I use both baking powder and bicarbonate of soda (baking soda) as rising agents in my cakes and desserts. Always buy aluminium-free products. Baking powder contains both an alkaline and acid and when it's mixed into the wet ingredients becomes activated. Bicarbonate of soda is an alkaline and needs an acid such as lemon juice for it to activate.

To thicken sauces or make creamy puddings, I tend to use kuzu or arrowroot and dissolve it in an equal amount of cold water before adding it to a boiling liquid. You need to stir the mixture continuously until the sauce becomes clear, then take the saucepan off the heat.

Agar agar acts like gelatine but is actually a sea vegetable. It comes in bars or flakes, but I find the flakes easier to use. Stir

into a boiling liquid, then simmer the mixture for 5 minutes until it dissolves. When the liquid cools it will set firm. For a variation, add kuzu or arrowroot to this liquid while it's still warm and you'll make a creamy mousse.

Spices such as cinnamon or cardamom not only accentuate the flavour of a dessert, but also help to create a more warming, heartfelt dish.

I always add a touch of unrefined sea salt to my sweets. This helps to draw all the ingredients together in a happy marriage to heighten the final flavour.

In my wet ingredients I include liquid sweeteners such as rice and barley syrup, fruit juice concentrate and maple syrup. Each has its own characteristic and behaves differently under different conditions. Rice syrup is a mild, middle-of-the-road, easy sweetener. Barley malt syrup by comparison is big and boisterous, packing a strong flavour with dark colouring. I buy either apple or pear juice concentrate, both made from the juice of fresh fruit that's been cooked down to create a more concentrated flavour. Then lastly, but never forgotten, I love to use premium grade maple syrup. This all-purpose favourite gives desserts a sweetness that will have you nodding with joy.

I include good-quality, easy to digest fats, such as unrefined coconut oil, hulled tahini and organic eggs. These not only give a great mouthfeel, but also add richness and moisture.

With milk I opt for an organic soy milk or almond milk. It gives desserts that luscious feel we long for in sweet treats.

To make silky-smooth creams and toppings, I use silken tofu which, when drained in a fine sieve to become firmer, forms the base of the dish. I then add some good-quality fat, a sweetener and flavouring before pureéing into a cream.

I always have some natural vanilla extract in the pantry as adding a few drops to a dessert creates another flavour and dimension.

Lemon, lime and orange zest are the threesome that give added zing to a cream creation or tang to a baked item. They are welcome in nearly all desserts, alone or in partnership.

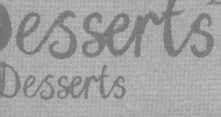

Carrot, cardamom and coconut cake

This cake creation has the scent of chai-spiced tea and is inspired by the traditional carrot halva dessert of India. The batter will also squeeze into a muffin tray making eight portable cupcakes to go.

Preheat the oven to 175°C (350°F/Gas Mark 4). Lightly oil a 22 cm (9 in) round cake tin and line the base and side with baking paper. Combine the spelt and coconut flours, baking powder, bicarbonate of soda, cardamom and a pinch of sea salt in a large bowl and whisk to aerate.

Mix the soy milk, maple syrup, coconut oil, orange blossom extract and lemon juice in a bowl. Pour into the dry ingredients and mix to form a smooth batter. Fold in the carrot, raisins and pistachios and stir to combine. Pour the mixture into the prepared cake tin and bake for 30 minutes, cooking for a further 20 minutes if necessary, until a skewer inserted into the centre of the cake comes out clean. Allow to cool for 30 minutes in the tin before turning out onto a wire rack to cool completely.

To make the frosting, bring the apricot, coconut cream and a pinch of sea salt to the boil in saucepan over high heat, then reduce the heat to medium and simmer for 7 minutes, or until the apricots have softened. Transfer to a food processor and process to make a smooth purée. Transfer back to a clean saucepan and bring to a simmer over medium heat. Add the kuzu mixture and simmer for 2 minutes, stirring to dissolve. Remove from the heat and stir in the lemon zest. Place in a bowl and refrigerate until cool.

Use a palette knife or a spatula to spread the frosting over the cake and sprinkle with the flaked coconut to serve.

Serves 8–10

1 cup spelt flour

1 cup coconut flour

1 teaspoon baking powder

1 teaspoon bicarbonate of soda (baking soda)

2 teaspoons ground cardamom

sea salt

½ cup soy milk

1 cup maple syrup or apple juice concentrate

2 tablespoons coconut oil (melted if solid)

2 drops orange blossom extract (optional)

3 tablespoons lemon juice

2 cups grated carrot

½ cup raisins

1 cup roughly chopped unsalted pistachios

COCONUT FROSTING

½ cup dried apricots, roughly chopped

270 ml (9¼ fl oz) coconut cream

sea salt

1 tablespoon kuzu or arrowroot dissolved in 1 tablespoon cold water

1 teaspoon finely grated lemon zest

½ cup flaked coconut, lightly toasted

Baked silken chocolate tart

This is my version of a baked chocolate cheesecake made with a rich, creamy almond butter. This tart is light and silky eaten on the day and if left overnight in the fridge will firm up nicely.

For the crust, put the ingredients in a food processor and process until the mixture comes together to form a ball. Wrap in plastic wrap and refrigerate for 30 minutes. When well rested, place the dough between two sheets of baking paper and roll out to a large circle with a 28 cm (11 in) diameter, about 3 mm (⅛ in) thick.

Preheat the oven to 180°C (350°F/Gas Mark 4). Lightly oil a 24 cm (9½ in) round tart tin and dust the base with 1 teaspoon flour. Place the pastry into the tin and press into the edges. Trim any excess pastry with a knife. Refrigerate for 10 minutes. Prick holes into the pastry base with a fork and line with a sheet of baking paper. Fill with some dried pulses and blind bake for 15 minutes. Remove the pulses and baking paper and continue to bake for a further 10 minutes. Allow to cool.

For the filling, put the ingredients in a food processor with a pinch of sea salt and process until the mixture is smooth, soft and creamy.

Pour the filling into the pastry case and cook in the oven for 20 minutes, or until firm to the touch. Cool for at least 15 minutes in the tin before removing. Serve cold, dusted with cocoa powder.

Serves 6

CRUST

1 cup unbleached white spelt flour

1 cup blanched almonds, roasted and ground

3 tablespoons coconut or macadamia oil

⅓ cup maple syrup

1 tablespoon cold water

pinch of sea salt

FILLING

600 g (1 lb 5 oz) silken tofu, drained in a fine sieve for 30 minutes

½ cup maple syrup or rice syrup

3 tablespoons almond butter or hulled tahini

100 g (3½ oz) organic dark cooking chocolate, melted

⅓ cup cocoa powder

finely grated zest of 1 orange

2 tablespoons kuzu or arrowroot

sea salt

Steamed mango, lime and coconut silk

This creamy citrus dessert uses silken tofu and is bursting with the tantalising tang of fresh mango. It is great served warm or chilled – a light and fresh, rapturous treat.

Put the silken tofu in a fine sieve and leave to drain for 30 minutes.

Preheat the oven to 175°C (350°F/Gas Mark 4). Put the tofu in a food processor with the coconut cream, palm sugar, lime juice and zest, kuzu, lemon oil, mango and a pinch of sea salt and process until smooth and silky. Spoon into six 125 ml (4 fl oz) ramekins, cover with foil and place in a roasting tin. Fill the tin with enough warm water to come halfway up the sides of the cups to create a steam bath. Place in the oven and cook for 30 minutes, or until slightly firm to the touch.

Top with shredded coconut and serve warm on a winter's night, or chilled in summer with a glass of sweet wine.

Serves 6

600 g (1 lb 5 oz) silken tofu
3 tablespoons coconut cream
3 tablespoons palm sugar (jaggery), grated
⅓ cup lime juice
finely grated zest of 2 limes
1 teaspoon kuzu or arrowroot
3 drops lemon oil
250 g (9 oz) mango, diced
sea salt
¼ cup shredded coconut

Steamed pear, date and ginger couscous cake

This isn't a cake in the typical sense – it's prepared on the stove rather than in the oven. The good thing about this is that you have complete control during the cooking process. This really is an 'anything goes' pudding, which means when you have an excess of seasonal stone fruit, such as fresh plums or apricots, use them instead of the pears. This is a great lunchbox snack or you can also try it steamed for breakfast.

To make the orange soy cream, put the ingredients in a food processor with a pinch of sea salt and process for 3 minutes, or until the mixture is smooth and creamy. Refrigerate for 1 hour. Keep any leftover cream refrigerated for up to 3 days.

Lightly grease a 19 cm (7½ in) cake tin or glass dish with oil. Bring the apple juice to the boil in a saucepan over medium heat. Add the star anise, cinnamon, pears, dates and a pinch of sea salt. Cover and simmer for 7 minutes, or until the pears are soft. Remove the star anise and add the rice syrup, ginger juice, lemon zest and vanilla, stirring for 1 minute. Pour in the couscous and simmer over low heat for 3–5 minutes, or until all the liquid has been absorbed. Spoon into the prepared tin and allow to cool and set for at least 15 minutes before turning out.

To make the glaze, put the orange juice and jam in a saucepan and stir with a whisk as you bring it to the boil. Add the kuzu mixture and stir continuously as the mixture thickens and becomes clear. Remove from the heat and spoon over the couscous cake.

Sprinkle the flaked almonds over the top, cut into slices and serve with orange soy cream.

Serves 6

Note: Grate a 4 cm (1½ in) knob of ginger, place in a muslin cloth (cheesecloth) and squeeze out the juice.

ORANGE SOY CREAM

300 g (10½ oz) silken tofu

2 tablespoons hulled tahini or almond butter

2 tablespoons maple syrup

1 teaspoon natural vanilla extract

1 tablespoon finely grated orange zest

sea salt

5 cups apple or pear juice

3 star anise

1 teaspoon ground cinnamon

2 beurre bosc pears, cored and finely sliced

½ cup pitted dates, chopped

sea salt

3 tablespoons rice syrup

1 tablespoon ginger juice (see Note)

finely grated zest of 1 lemon

1 teaspoon natural vanilla extract

2 cups couscous

½ cup orange juice or water

3 tablespoons strawberry jam

2 teaspoons kuzu or arrowroot dissolved in 2 teaspoons cold water

¼ cup toasted flaked almonds

Apple and cranberry pudding with orange syrup

This is a classic autumn day dessert. Simply make a cake batter, fold in the fruit and steam under pressure. Alternate the fruit if you wish, trying fresh apricots or blood plums instead of the cranberries.

Combine the coconut flour, spelt flour, bicarbonate of soda, baking powder, cinnamon, allspice and a pinch of sea salt in a large bowl and whisk to aerate.

In a separate bowl, combine the apple juice, soy milk, rice syrup, orange zest and vanilla and whisk to combine. Fold into the flour mixture with a wooden spoon until just combined. Fold in the diced apples, cranberries and walnuts and mix well.

Lightly oil two 500 ml (17 fl oz) pudding tins and line with muslin (cheesecloth). Spoon the mixture evenly between each tin. Cover the top of each with a square of baking paper, then wrap a piece of foil tightly over the top, securing the 'lids' with kitchen string.

Place the puddings in a large, deep saucepan and pour in enough hot water to come two-thirds up the side of the tins – you may need to do this in two batches. Bring the water to the boil, cover the saucepan with a tight-fitting lid and simmer over low heat for 90 minutes, making sure the water level is kept high and re-filling as needed. Allow to cool for 15 minutes, then turn out onto plates.

To make the glaze, bring the orange juice and maple syrup to the boil in a saucepan over high heat. Add the kuzu mixture to the pan and stir for 2 minutes, or until the syrup is thick and clear. Ladle the glaze over each pudding. Serve warm or at room temperature.

Makes 2 puddings

1 cup coconut flour or wholemeal spelt flour

1 cup unbleached spelt flour

1 teaspoon bicarbonate of soda (baking soda)

1 teaspoon baking powder

½ teaspoon ground cinnamon

½ teaspoon ground allspice

sea salt

¾ cup apple juice

3 tablespoons soy milk

½ cup rice syrup or maple syrup

2 teaspoons finely grated orange zest

¼ teaspoon natural vanilla extract

2 apples, peeled, cored and diced

1 cup cranberries (fresh or frozen)

1 cup toasted and chopped walnuts

GLAZE

½ cup orange juice

½ cup maple syrup

1 teaspoon kuzu or arrowroot dissolved in 1 teaspoon cold water

Hazelnut and mocha budino

This mousse-like dessert is refreshing and luscious. Make it the day before and enjoy at the end of a banquet. Keep refrigerated – for up to three days – otherwise it may melt slightly. If you wish, you can use regular espresso coffee instead of the grain coffee.

To make the candied orange peel, cut the orange peel into ribbons, removing any white pith. Bring a small saucepan of water to the boil and blanch the peel for 1 minute, then remove and refresh in a bowl of cold water. Blanch twice more to remove any bitterness. Put 3 tablespoons water and the rice syrup in a small saucepan and bring to the boil. Add the orange zest and simmer over low heat for 20 minutes. Allow to cool and store in an airtight jar until needed.

Preheat the oven to 170°C (340°F/Gas Mark 3). To make the hazelnut praline, put the hazelnuts on a baking tray and bake for 5 minutes. Allow to cool slightly, rub off the skins and transfer the nuts to a small bowl. Pour on the rice and maple syrups and mix well. Transfer to a baking tray lined with baking paper and bake for 15 minutes, or until they begin to smell sweet. Cool and store in an airtight container in a cool, dry place.

Bring the grain coffee and 1½ cups water to the boil in a saucepan over high heat. Reduce the heat to medium and simmer for 7 minutes, or until the liquid reduces to 1 cup. Strain into a separate saucepan and add the soy milk, agar agar, rice syrup, maple syrup and a pinch of sea salt. Bring to the boil, then reduce the heat and simmer for 3–4 minutes, stirring until the agar agar flakes dissolve. Add the kuzu mixture to the pan and stir until the mixture begins to thicken. Remove from the heat and add the ground hazelnuts, tahini, orange zest and vanilla. Pour into six 125 ml (4 fl oz) ramekins. Allow to cool, then serve with candied orange peel and hazelnut praline.

Makes 6

CANDIED ORANGE PEEL
1 orange
3 tablespoons rice syrup

HAZELNUT PRALINE
½ cup hazelnuts
1 tablespoon rice syrup
1 tablespoon maple syrup

⅓ cup grain coffee (found in most health food shops)
3 cups soy or almond milk
1 tablespoon agar agar flakes
½ cup rice syrup
3 tablespoons maple syrup
sea salt
2 tablespoons kuzu or arrowroot dissolved in 2 tablespoons cold water
1 cup hazelnuts, roasted, skinned and finely ground
2 tablespoons hulled tahini or almond butter
1 teaspoon finely grated orange zest
1 teaspoon natural vanilla extract

Chilled
raspberry kanten

This raspberry jelly makes a refreshing summer treat. Mix and match fresh fruits and fruit juices to suit your fancy. Enjoy it at the end of a feast to soothe the day away, or try feeding it to overheated children and watch them chill out and relax.

Bring the fruit juice, agar agar and a pinch of sea salt to the boil in a saucepan over medium heat. Simmer for 5 minutes, stirring until the agar agar completely dissolves. Add the lemon juice, zest and vanilla, stir to combine, then remove from the heat.

Arrange the raspberries in the base of four serving glasses and gently pour the juice mixture over the fruit. Allow to stand at room temperature or refrigerate for 30 minutes to set. Serve with mint leaves, if desired.

Serves 4

3 cups clear apple juice
   or pink moscato
3 teaspoons agar agar flakes
sea salt
1 tablespoon lemon juice
finely grated zest of 1 lemon
¼ teaspoon natural vanilla
   extract
2 cups raspberries, rinsed
1 tablespoon finely sliced mint
   leaves (optional)

Polenta, plum and almond torta

This cake is inspired from the Italian peasant polenta (cornmeal) cakes that I sampled while vespa-ing around Italy. My version includes fat, ripe plums, but feel free to substitute with a handful of fresh raspberries or ripe figs. Make sure you purchase fine polenta or the instant variety, as the coarse version will have you visiting your dentist!

Preheat the oven to 170°C (340°F/Gas Mark 3). Lightly oil a 22 cm (9 in) round cake tin and line the base and side with baking paper. Combine the flour, polenta, baking powder, bicarbonate of soda and a pinch of sea salt in a large bowl and whisk to aerate.

Combine the orange juice, oil, maple syrup, orange and lemon zests and vanilla in a separate bowl and whisk to combine. Pour this into the flour mixture and stir well until a smooth batter forms.

Pour the batter into the prepared tin. Arrange the plum halves, cut side down, in the batter and sprinkle the flaked almonds over any exposed batter.

Bake in the oven for 45 minutes, or until a skewer inserted into the centre of the cake comes out clean. Cool for 15 minutes in the tin before turning out onto a wire rack to cool completely before serving.

Serves 8

- 2 cups unbleached white flour or spelt flour
- 1 cup fine or instant polenta (cornmeal)
- 2 teaspoons baking powder
- 2 teaspoons bicarbonate of soda (baking soda)
- sea salt
- 1 cup orange juice
- 3 tablespoons light olive oil
- 1 cup maple syrup or pear juice concentrate
- finely grated zest of 1 orange
- finely grated zest of 1 lemon
- 1 teaspoon natural vanilla extract
- 3 ripe blood plums, halved, stones removed
- ½ cup flaked almonds

Lemon, almond and grape cake

This cake was inspired by my mother. It came at a time when all of my baked goods seemed to be flavoured with lemons – even while my mum's vines dripped with plump red grapes. She thought the tasty fruit would look pretty on my birthday cake – and the flavour was perfect – so a new cake was born. Here is the latest version of this well-loved wholesome treat.

Preheat the oven to 180°C (350°F/Gas Mark 4). Grease a 22 cm (9 in) round cake tin and line the base and side with baking paper. Remove the grapes from the stem and roll in the pear juice concentrate. Place on a baking tray and bake for 5 minutes, or until the grapes wilt slightly. Remove from the oven and set aside.

Whisk together the flour, ground almonds and bicarbonate of soda in a bowl and set aside.

In a separate bowl, whisk together the oil, pear juice concentrate, eggs, vanilla, lemon juice and zest. Gradually fold in the dry ingredients and stir well to combine. Pour the cake batter into the prepared tin and arrange the roasted grapes on top.

Bake for 40 minutes, or until a skewer inserted into the centre of the cake comes out clean. Allow to cool for 30 minutes in the tin before turning out. Serve warm.

Serves 8

ROASTED GRAPES

250 g (9 oz) seedless red grapes

1 tablespoon pear juice concentrate

1½ cups spelt flour

1 cup ground almonds

2 teaspoons bicarbonate of soda (baking soda)

½ cup light olive oil or rice bran oil

1 cup pear or apple juice concentrate

3 eggs

1 teaspoon natural vanilla extract

⅔ cup lemon juice

finely grated zest of 1 lemon

Sauces, pickles & condiments

SAUCES

Sauces draw ingredients together and breathe freshness and life into a dish. They give meals their distinctive character and help support all the ingredients into becoming a happy, cohesive dish. We all know when a meal feels satisfying and most often it's the sauce that makes it happen.

My repertoire includes three styles of sauces. Firstly there are the clear sauces, which are thickened with either kuzu or arrowroot, and used to glaze noodles. These dishes all look smooth and satin-like and taste fantastic with the clear glaze holding the ingredients and flavours together.

The second style is a puréed vegetable sauce, often made from slow-cooked sweet vegetables and then blended until creamy. Puréed pumpkin or carrot are then enriched with tahini or olive oil to make a satisfying sauce. Use over vegetables, with noodles or grains, or as a dip.

The third style of sauce is uncooked, and basically a dressing. Whisk together an oil and vinegar combination, or blend together some tahini and lemon juice. All dressings must have a fat component, such as olive oil, sesame oil or tahini, combined with something acidic such as vinegar or a citrus juice. Add sea salt and a herb like basil or chives, whisk and serve. Dressings keep well when sealed in a jar and refrigerated.

Sauces and dressings explode with excitement and taste when you use a combination of the following flavours: sour – lemon, lime, vinegar, yoghurt; bitter – olive oil, sesame oil, tahini, toasted sesame seeds; sweet – rice syrup, mirin, honey; pungent – ginger, garlic, horseradish, mustard; salty – miso, sea salt, shoyu, tamari.

PICKLES

Pickles are often forgotten on the plate, pushed aside or hardly noticed. Natural pickles are nature's way of delivering live enzymes into the gut to aid good digestion. Pickles set about restoring the intestinal flora by promoting the growth of healthy bacteria. So for some, pickles may be a bit of a miracle food, or at least a good pick-me-up, but beware, eat small amounts as pickles contain a fair amount of unrefined sea salt.

Most cultures boast about their own time-honoured method of making a particular pickle. Generally, pickles have evolved within cultures where they've needed to preserve foods for the whole year. The Japanese delight in a little pickle with their fried foods. The Germans munch on sauerkraut, the Polish enjoy pickled cucumber and the Italians have their *giardiniere*.

Pickles come in two styles: 'quick to pickle' or 'long to pickle'.

Some quick pickle varieties are also called pressed salads. By combining crisp, firm vegetables with unrefined sea salt and adding some weight for up to an hour you will produce a simple pickle. The pressing action breaks down the cellulose in the vegetables making nutrients available. If your pickle turns out too salty, rinse the vegetables under cold running water, squeeze out the excess water and serve.

CONDIMENTS

Condiments are great for adding a little extra seasoning for those who need it with their meal. By combining unrefined sea salt with toasted seeds you add extra minerals to your dish. Beware – they're addictive!

Sauces,
pickles & condiments Sau
pickles & c

Italian red sauce

This is a traditional red sauce that one of my cooking teachers was kind enough to share. I've added and subtracted ingredients to create my own flavour. You can use it as a pasta sauce or for the base of a pizza. If you find that it is a little watery, bring the puréed sauce to the boil and thicken it with 1 teaspoon of kuzu or arrowroot dissolved in 1 teaspoon water. If you're in the mood, make lots and freeze it for up to one month or refrigerate for up to three days.

Heat 1 tablespoon oil in a heavy-based saucepan over medium heat and sauté the onion and garlic for 3–4 minutes, or until softened. Add the carrot, pumpkin, beetroot and celery with just enough water to cover the vegetables (use vegetable stock if you prefer), and season lightly with sea salt. Add the bay leaf, cover, and bring to the boil, then reduce the heat to low and simmer for 25 minutes, or until the vegetables have softened and the sauce has reduced.

Remove the pan from the heat and allow to cool. Discard the bay leaf and transfer the sauce ingredients to a food processor. Process to make a smooth purée. Return the sauce to a clean saucepan, adjust the seasoning by adding the umeboshi paste and freshly ground black pepper. Add the basil and stir in the remaining oil. Serve warm.

Makes 2 cups

3 tablespoons extra virgin olive oil

1 onion, sliced

1 garlic clove, crushed

1 carrot, chopped

200 g (7 oz) pumpkin, peeled and cubed

50 g (1¾ oz) beetroot (beet), peeled and diced

2 celery stalks, diced

sea salt

1 bay leaf

1 teaspoon umeboshi paste

¼ teaspoon freshly ground black pepper

2 tablespoons roughly chopped basil leaves

Pumpkin, orange and tahini sauce

This creamy purée works well over polenta, millet or rice and is just as good over pasta. Serve warm or cold as a tasty dip. Make a double batch and freeze some for a lazy day. Refrigerate for up to three days.

Place the pumpkin, onion and a pinch of sea salt in a steamer over a saucepan of boiling water and steam for 15 minutes, or until the pumpkin has softened. Remove from the heat and transfer to a food processor with the tahini, ginger juice and orange zest. Process to make a smooth purée and serve.

Makes 2 cups

Note: Grate a 1 cm (½ in) knob of ginger, place in a muslin cloth (cheesecloth) and squeeze out the juice.

400 g (14 oz) pumpkin, peeled and chopped

1 onion, chopped

sea salt

2 tablespoons hulled tahini

1 teaspoon ginger juice (see Note)

1 teaspoon finely grated orange zest

Sweet and sour sauce

This clear and sticky sauce will make a meal exciting in minutes. Pour it hot over cooked udon or buckwheat (soba) noodles, tofu and tempeh stir-fries, or over a bowl of steamed vegetables. You can also try adding some coriander (cilantro) leaves or toasted sesame seeds for a different effect. Refrigerate for up to three days.

Bring the apple juice, shoyu, rice vinegar and syrup to the boil in a saucepan over high heat. Whisk in the kuzu mixture for 2–3 minutes, or until the sauce thickens. Remove from the heat and add the ginger juice before serving.

Makes ¾ cup

Note: Grate a 1 cm (½ in) knob of ginger, place in a muslin cloth (cheesecloth) and squeeze out the juice.

½ cup apple juice

⅓ cup shoyu

2 tablespoons brown rice vinegar

⅓ cup brown rice syrup or barley malt

1 teaspoon kuzu or arrowroot dissolved in 1 teaspoon cold water

1 teaspoon ginger juice (see Note)

Onion shiitake sauce

This robust sauce goes well with grilled (broiled) tofu or tempeh steaks or as a gravy over polenta or millet. Serve hot. Store any leftover sauce in the refrigerator for 3 days.

Drain the shiitake mushrooms, reserving the soaking liquid. Remove the stems and thinly slice the caps. Set aside.

Heat the sesame oil in a heavy-based frying pan over low heat and sauté the onion for 5 minutes, or until soft and translucent. Add the shiitake soaking liquid, mushrooms, mirin and shoyu and simmer for 10 minutes. Add the kuzu mixture, stirring for 2 minutes, or until the sauce thickens. Remove from the heat, then stir through the spring onion and ginger juice to serve.

Makes 1 cup

Note: Grate a 4 cm (1½ in) knob of ginger, place in a muslin cloth (cheesecloth) and squeeze out the juice.

10 dried shiitake mushrooms, soaked overnight in 1 cup water

1 tablespoon dark roasted sesame oil

2 onions, finely sliced

2 tablespoons mirin

2 tablespoons shoyu

1 cup water

3 teaspoons kuzu or arrowroot, dissolved in 3 teaspoons cold water

2 tablespoons finely sliced spring onions (scallions)

1 tablespoon ginger juice (see Note)

Carrot butter

This exciting vegetable purée is simple to make, sweet-tasting and easy to digest. I thin it out with orange juice to create a runny sauce, but you can keep it thick to smear over toast or use as a dip. Spice it up with a teaspoon of ground cumin and freshly chopped coriander (cilantro) leaves if you wish. Refrigerate for up to three days.

Heat the oil in a heavy-based saucepan over medium heat and sauté the onion and garlic for 2 minutes. Add the carrot and sauté for a further 3 minutes, or until lightly browned. Add the orange juice and umeboshi paste, cover, and simmer for 15 minutes, or until the carrots are soft. Stir in the mirin, then transfer to a food processor and process to create a creamy butter.

Makes 2 cups

1 tablespoon olive oil

¼ onion, diced

2 garlic cloves, crushed

2 carrots, diced

½ cup orange juice

1 teaspoon umeboshi paste

1 tablespoon mirin

Roast capsicum and black olive sauce

This sauce adds flavour and excitement to your meals – serve it over any grain or noodle dish, add a dollop to a bean soup or polenta or simply spread onto a slice of crusty bread. It tastes great slightly warmed or can be served cold. Refrigerate for up to three days.

1 red capsicum (pepper)

10 pitted black olives, roughly chopped

1 garlic clove, crushed

2 tablespoons roughly chopped basil leaves

30 g (1 oz) ground almonds or breadcrumbs

½ small hot chilli, seeds removed and chopped (optional)

⅓ cup extra virgin olive oil

2 tablespoons red wine vinegar

sea salt and freshly ground black pepper

Preheat the oven to 200°C (400°F/Gas Mark 6). Roast the capsicum for 15 minutes, or until the skin is blackened. Remove from the oven and place in a plastic bag. Leave to cool for 20 minutes, then remove the skin and seeds. Drain for 5 minutes, then chop the flesh and place in a food processor with the remaining ingredients. Process to create a smooth purée. Gently reheat in a clean saucepan if serving warm.

Makes 1 cup

Fresh broad bean pesto

This fresh green pesto makes a perfect dip or it can be mixed into pasta dishes or spooned over soups. Try substituting the broad (fava) beans with blanched broccoli, asparagus or fresh peas. Serve slightly warm or at room temperature. Refrigerate for up to three days.

250 g (9 oz) shelled broad (fava) beans

1 garlic clove, crushed

3 tablespoons roasted pine nuts

1 large handful roughly chopped basil leaves

3 tablespoons extra virgin olive oil

150 g (5½ oz) silken tofu

2 teaspoons white miso

1 teaspoon finely grated lemon zest

¼ teaspoon freshly ground black pepper

Bring a small saucepan of water to the boil. Drop in the fresh broad beans and cook for 3–5 minutes, or until softened. Drain and refresh immediately under cold running water. Peel the outer skins and discard.

Place the broad beans, garlic and pine nuts in a food processor and process until the mixture resembles breadcrumbs. Add the basil, oil, tofu, miso, lemon zest and freshly ground black pepper and process to make a smooth purée.

Makes 1½ cups

Orange, sesame and ginger dressing

The sesame oil gives this dressing a strong Asian accent, which is great in noodle salads. Allow the noodles to marinate for at least 30 minutes prior to eating to really develop the flavour. Refrigerate for up to one week.

Whisk all the dressing ingredients together in a bowl and refrigerate until ready to use.

Makes ¾ cup

Note: Grate a 4 cm (1½ in) knob of ginger, place in a muslin cloth (cheesecloth) and squeeze out the juice.

½ cup orange juice

1 tablespoon orange zest

1 tablespoon ginger juice (see Note)

1 teaspoon brown rice vinegar

½ teaspoon soy sauce

1 teaspoon dark sesame oil

Warm red onion, tomato and basil vinaigrette

I serve this dressing with steamed fish, and it also works well over millet or quinoa grains – pour it over while the grains are still warm and allow them to absorb the flavours. Refrigerate for up to three days.

Simmer the olive oil, vinegar, onion, tomato and olives in a saucepan over low heat for 3 minutes, or until the onion and tomato soften slightly. Just before serving add the lemon juice and basil and serve warm.

Makes 1 cup

3 tablespoons extra virgin olive oil

3 tablespoons balsamic or red wine vinegar

¼ red (Spanish) onion, diced

½ tomato, seeds removed and diced

6 pitted black olives, sliced

2 tablespoons lemon juice

2 tablespoons roughly chopped basil leaves

Silken mayonnaise

This is a lighter version of mayonnaise, with an excellent mouthfeel and fine, lemony flavour. It works well over blanched vegetables or served with grilled (broiled) fish or chicken. Refrigerate before serving for up to three days.

Put all of the ingredients into a food processor and process until smooth and creamy. Cover and refrigerate until ready to use.

Makes 1 cup

300 g (10½ oz) silken tofu

1 tablespoon extra virgin olive oil

1 tablespoon lemon juice

1 teaspoon dijon mustard

2 teaspoons finely grated lemon zest

¼ teaspoon ground turmeric

¼ teaspoon sea salt

¼ teaspoon freshly ground black pepper

2 teaspoons white miso

2 teaspoons brown rice syrup

Sweet lemon tahini sauce

This everyday dressing is delicious smothered over fresh or blanched greens and can be served warm or cold. You can also spoon it over grain dishes for that extra tang. Add a teaspoon of freshly grated ginger juice for some added warmth and spice. Refrigerate for up to three days.

Put all of the ingredients into a food processor and process until smooth and creamy. Add extra water or lemon juice to make a pouring consistency, if needed.

Makes 1 cup

½ cup hulled tahini

⅔ cup lemon juice

1 teaspoon honey

1 teaspoon umeboshi paste

1 teaspoon finely grated ginger

½ cup roughly chopped flat-leaf (Italian) parsley

sea salt and freshly ground black pepper

Horseradish salsa

This pungent dressing is a good coating for boiled beetroot (beet), pumpkin or sweet potatoes as its strong flavour needs a hardy backdrop. Serve it cold and refrigerate any leftover salsa for up to three days.

Put all of the ingredients into a food processor and process to combine well. The mixture will have a grainy texture. Cover and refrigerate until ready to use.

Makes 1 cup

250 g (9 oz) plain yoghurt

4 cm (1½ in) knob of horseradish, finely chopped, or 1 tablespoon horseradish paste

freshly squeezed juice of 1 lemon

finely grated zest of 1 orange

1 tablespoon extra virgin olive oil

1 teaspoon ground cumin

1 tablespoon finely chopped coriander (cilantro) leaves

pinch of sea salt

pinch of freshly ground black pepper

Coconut cream sauce

Use this sauce as the base for a Thai-inspired curry – simply add tofu and vegetables, fish or chicken to make a tasty dish. Adjust the chilli according to your heat tolerance. Make lots and freeze it, or store in the refrigerator for up to three days. Always serve warm and reheat gently, while stirring, to bring the sauce back to a suitable temperature before adding any other ingredients.

Put all of the ingredients in a food processor and process until smooth and creamy. Heat a heavy-based saucepan over medium heat, add the paste and stir for 3–5 minutes, or until all the ingredients are softened and the liquid is reduced. Once fragrant, add the kaffir lime leaves and ½ cup water. Simmer for 15 minutes, then pour in the coconut cream and a little sea salt and continue to simmer for about 3 minutes. Add the lemon juice just before serving.

Makes 1 cup

PASTE

1 onion, diced

1 tablespoon chopped ginger

1 teaspoon chopped fresh turmeric or ½ teaspoon ground turmeric

1 tablespoon chopped galangal

4 cm (1½ in) stem lemongrass, bruised and finely chopped

1 garlic clove, minced

¼ red chilli, sliced

8 coriander (cilantro) roots, rinsed and finely chopped

2 kaffir lime leaves

400 ml (14 fl oz) coconut cream

sea salt

2 teaspoons lemon juice

Chilli dressing

2 tablespoons orange juice

1 tablespoon dark roasted
sesame oil

1 teaspoon shoyu

2 tablespoons rice vinegar

1 tablespoon mirin

1 teaspoon finely grated
orange zest

½ chilli, seeds removed
and finely chopped

**This dressing is spicy hot, so is best
used on a robust bean or pasta salad. Try
substituting a teaspoon of smoked paprika
or add it as well as the chilli for a smoky
effect. Refrigerate for up to one week.**

Combine the ingredients in a bowl and
whisk together.

Makes ½ cup

Parsley dressing

⅓ cup extra virgin olive oil

3 tablespoons lemon juice

1 tablespoon brown rice vinegar

1 garlic clove, crushed

1 teaspoon dijon mustard

½ cup roughly chopped flat-leaf
(Italian) parsley

finely grated zest of 1 lemon

¼ teaspoon sea salt

**This green, garlicky lemon dressing is
great as a marinade for beans and pasta
salads. Its creaminess is perfect with
steamed asparagus or green beans.
Refrigerate for up to three days.**

Put all of the ingredients into a food
processor and process until smooth
and creamy.

Makes ½ cup

Pickled ginger

7 cm (3 in) knob of ginger,
  finely sliced
1 teaspoon sea salt
½ cup brown rice vinegar
1 tablespoon rice syrup
1 tablespoon beetroot (beet) juice

**Have you ever wondered how to make
your own pickled ginger? Here's my
sugar-free version. Pickled ginger aids
in the digestion of oils, so is a great
accompaniment to any fried food. You can
also chop it into salads, dressings or enjoy
it alongside fish dishes. It's best to make
this pickle with fresh, tender green ginger,
which is available in autumn.**

Put the ginger into a stainless steel bowl.
Add the salt, toss and leave for 1 hour. Rinse
off the salt and dry the ginger slices with
paper towel before packing them into
a sterilised, airtight jar.

Bring the rice vinegar and syrup to the
boil in a saucepan over high heat. Add the
beetroot juice, then quickly pour the mixture
over the ginger. Allow to cool, then store in
the refrigerator. Store the ginger for at least
5 days before using.

Makes ½ cup

Pickled onions

250 g (9 oz) small (pearl/pickling)
  onions or French shallots
2 teaspoons umeboshi vinegar

**To make this pickle even more quickly,
finely slice the onions and blanch for
3 minutes before adding the umeboshi
vinegar. Use pickled onions in salads or
grain dishes for their beauty and sour
flavour. If they become too sour or salty
stir in half a teaspoon of rice syrup.**

Bring a small saucepan of water to the
boil and add the onions. Cook until soft,
then remove from the heat and drain well.
Transfer to a bowl and add the umeboshi
vinegar, stirring occasionally. Allow to cool,
then refrigerate. Use within 3 days.

Makes 1 cup

Red radish pickles

These radish pickles look great on a plate and are sweet, salty and sour to taste. Refrigerate for up to three days.

Bring the radishes, vinegar and 3 tablespoons water to the boil in a saucepan over high heat. Cover, reduce the heat and simmer for 10 minutes, or until the radishes are soft. Reduce the liquid enough to just glaze the radishes. Serve sprinkled with the orange zest.

Makes 1 cup

250 g (9 oz) red radishes, stems removed
1 tablespoon umeboshi vinegar
1 teaspoon orange zest

Cucumber and fresh dill pickle

This is a refreshing addition to a rich meal and only takes minutes to make. If you like, add mint or parsley instead of dill. Refrigerate for up to three days.

Combine the cucumber and sea salt in a bowl. Transfer to a pickle press or onto a flat surface and cover with a plate topped by a weight and press for 30–60 minutes.

Check the taste and, if too salty, rinse and squeeze out the excess moisture. Stir in the dill and serve.

Makes 1½ cups

2 cups finely sliced cucumber
1 teaspoon sea salt
1 teaspoon roughly chopped dill

Pressed Chinese cabbage and friends

This is my adaptation of the traditional Korean kimchee pickle recipe. The longer the vegetables remain pressed under the salt, the more pickled they become and the more intense the flavour. Serve with grains, fish or chicken.

Combine all the ingredients in a bowl. Transfer to a pickle press or onto a flat surface and cover with a plate topped by a weight and press for 30–60 minutes. Drain off any excess liquid and serve.

Makes 1½ cups

150 g (5½ oz) Chinese cabbage, shredded

150 g (5½ oz) mustard greens, finely chopped

½ carrot, cut into matchsticks

¼ daikon radish, cut into matchsticks

¼ red (Spanish) onion, finely sliced

¼ teaspoon finely chopped ginger

1 tablespoon coriander (cilantro) leaves

1 teaspoon freshly grated lime zest

¼ teaspoon chilli, seeds removed and finely chopped

2 teaspoons sea salt

Carrot and daikon pickle

This great and simple pickle goes especially well with fish dishes. The texture is crunchy and satisfying. Refrigerate for up to three days.

Combine the carrot, daikon and sea salt in a bowl. Transfer to a pickle press or onto a flat surface and cover with a plate topped by a weight and press for 30–60 minutes. Drain off any excess liquid and stir in the vinegar and mirin. Serve with the toasted sesame seeds on top.

Makes 1½ cups

1 carrot, cut into fine matchsticks

½ daikon, cut into fine matchsticks

1 teaspoon sea salt

1 teaspoon brown rice vinegar

1 teaspoon mirin

1 teaspoon toasted sesame seeds

Sesame and wakame condiment

This black, mildly salty condiment is a storehouse of iron and iodine. Use for its dramatic look and flavour on top of greens, grains and salads.

60 g (2 oz) wakame seaweed
¼ cup sesame seeds, rinsed and drained

Preheat the oven to 170°C (340°F/Gas Mark 3). Bake the wakame on a baking tray for 5 minutes, or until dark and crunchy. Allow to cool, then place in a mortar or a spice grinder and pound with a pestle or grind to a fine powder.

Dry-fry the sesame seeds in a shallow frying pan over medium heat for 5 minutes, or until the seeds begin to brown and pop. Remove from the heat.

Place the sesame seeds in a mortar or a spice grinder and pound with a pestle or grind until roughly crushed. Combine with the wakame powder and store in an airtight container. Keep in a dry, cool place for up to 3 weeks.

Makes ½ cup

Nut and seed condiment

This spicy mixture will add a touch of the Orient to a grain, bean or greens dish. It also tastes superb sprinkled over cooked fish or chicken.

80 g (2¾ oz) hazelnuts
40 g (1½ oz)cumin seeds
40 g (1½ oz) coriander seeds
40 g (1½ oz) sesame seeds
1 teaspoon coarse sea salt

Preheat the oven to 160°C (320°F/Gas Mark 2–3). Roast the hazelnuts on a baking tray for 7 minutes, or until golden. Remove from the oven and allow to cool. Rub the skins off, place in a mortar or a spice grinder and roughly pound with a pestle or grind.

Roast the seeds separately in the oven for 5 minutes each, or until golden and fragrant. Allow to cool, then add to the hazelnuts with the sea salt. Grind the mixture until you get a coarse crumb-like texture. Allow to cool, then store in an airtight container for up to 3 weeks.

Makes 1½ cups

Sesame salt

This sesame salt is not only a calcium and iron boost but it tastes great too. It's perfect sprinkled over grains, beans and salads.

Dry-fry the sea salt in a shallow frying pan over medium heat for 5 minutes, or until it changes in colour from white to grey. Remove from the heat and transfer to a mortar.

Dry-fry the sesame seeds in a shallow frying pan over medium heat for 5 minutes, or until the seeds begin to brown and pop. Remove from the heat and add to the mortar with the salt.

Grind the sesame seeds and salt together with a pestle until the seeds are half crushed. Allow to cool and store in an airtight container. Keep in a dry, cool place for up to 3 weeks.

Makes ½ cup

1 teaspoon coarse sea salt

20 teaspoons hulled sesame seeds or black sesame seeds, rinsed and drained

Soy-toasted seeds

Loaded with great fats, these seeds go well over greens, salads and all grain dishes.

Rinse the pumpkin seeds in a fine strainer, drain and add to a frying pan over medium heat. Stir constantly until the seeds begin to brown and pop. Sprinkle with shoyu and stir to coat. Remove from the heat and transfer to a bowl.

Clean the pan and reheat over medium heat. Dry-fry the sunflower and sesame seeds separately for 5 minutes each, or until golden, then add some shoyu and transfer all the seeds into the one bowl. Toss the seeds together and allow to cool. Place in an airtight container and keep in a dry, cool place for up to 3 weeks.

Makes 1 cup

⅓ cup pumpkin seeds (pepitas)

3–4 drops shoyu

⅓ cup sunflower seeds

⅓ cup sesame seeds

Glossary

adzuki beans – a small, dark red bean low in fat, sometimes called azuki or aduki.

agar agar – a clear gelatin derived from a species of sea vegetable. Available in flake, bar or powder form. Used for making jelly-style desserts.

almond butter – a paste made from ground almonds. High in monounsaturated fats and a good source of protein, potassium, calcium and iron.

arrowroot – a starch flour processed from a tuber, similar to cornflour (cornstarch) or kuzu. Used as a thickening agent. Dissolve arrowroot with a cold liquid before adding to a hot liquid.

balsamic vinegar – aged, dark syrupy vinegar with a subtle sweetness. Great mixed with bitter greens.

barley malt – a thick, dark syrup used as a sweetener. It is made by sprouting and fermenting whole barley.

black sesame seeds – small black seeds, toasted and used as a garnish or for sesame salt.

buckwheat – although used as a grain, is a member of the rhubarb family. Use in pilafs or salads, or try making buckwheat flour pancakes.

chickpeas (garbanzo beans) – traditionally used in Middle Eastern cookery. Soak dried chickpeas the night before cooking.

coconut cream – thick coconut milk that is extracted by passing coconut meat through a fine grater and squeezing.

coconut flour – a low-carb, high-fibre, gluten-free alternative to wheat flour that also tastes great.

coconut oil – search for an extra virgin coconut oil, which is a pure, natural, unrefined oil derived from fresh coconut. It is clear and aromatic, with a mild, natural flavour.

cornmeal – also known as maize or polenta, ranges from finely ground to coarse.

couscous – partially refined cracked wheat. Steam to cook.

daikon – a long white radish. Used in Japanese-style soups and casseroles. Grated raw, it helps the digestion of oil or fish.

ginger – a spicy, tan-coloured root which creates warmth throughout the body when added to dishes. To make ginger juice, grate and squeeze through a piece of muslin cloth (cheesecloth).

kombu – a wide, thick, dark green sea vegetable. Use in soups, bean dishes and as a condiment.

kuzu – a white starch powder made from the root of a wild mountain plant; also known as kudzu. Used to thicken sauces, custards and desserts. Dissolve kuzu with a cold liquid before adding to a hot liquid.

lemon oil – extract of lemon derived from lemon zest steeped in pure alcohol.

maple syrup – made by boiling down the sap from the maple tree until it's a thick, rich, golden syrup.

millet – a small, golden cereal grain. Choose hulled for everyday cooking.

mirin – a sweet cooking wine made from fermented white or brown rice.

miso – a fermented paste made from soy beans, sea salt and sometimes incorporated with barley, white rice and other grains. A seasoning for soups, dips and sauces.

nori – thin dried sheets of black or purple sea vegetable. Buy already toasted or toast over an open flame for a few seconds. Use as a garnish for soups or wrap around rice balls or sushi.

olive oil – extra virgin, virgin and cold-pressed are all different grades of extraction from olives, at different temperatures, which affects taste and properties.

palm sugar (jaggery) – a thick, crumbly, richly flavoured brown sugar from the sugar palm tree.

pomegranate molasses – a dark sticky liquid made from pomegranate juice reduction that is slightly sweet and tart.

preserved lemon – lemons which have been preserved in salt for up to 30 days. Acidic, salty and sweet, slice and use in dips, sauces and marinades.

quinoa – a seed from a wild grass that grows in the Andes in South America. A perfect protein; great in soups, salads and as a pilaf.

rice syrup – a natural sweetener, derived from sprouted fermented rice. Lighter in colour and flavour than barley malt.

rice vinegar – a clear, mild flavoured vinegar obtained from fermented white or brown rice.

sea salt – white or grey unrefined sea salt is obtained from evaporated sea water; rock salt is mined from the land. It may be sun-dried or baked in a kiln. High in trace elements and minerals.

sesame oil – a dark coloured, thick, aromatic oil made from roasted sesame seeds.

shiitake mushrooms – a variety of Japanese mushroom often bought dried. Soak for at least 2 hours then add to soups and stocks.

shoyu – shoyu is a variety of soy sauce traditionally made from whole soy beans, wheat, sea salt and water and naturally fermented for 2–3 years. Tamari is a wheat-free version.

silken tofu – thickened soy milk which has a smooth and delicate texture. Best puréed into soups, dips, sauces and sweet creams.

soba noodles – noodles made from buckwheat flour, or sometimes buckwheat flour combined with wholewheat flour.

spelt – an ancient cereal grain that has a mellow, nutty flavour and is easy to digest. Use spelt flour to replace white flour in traditional recipes.

split peas – the two most popular varieties are yellow and green. They don't need soaking and, when cooked, melt to make hearty soups or purées.

tahini – a seed butter obtained by grinding sesame seeds until smooth and creamy. Hulled tahini is lighter in colour and more bitter, while unhulled tahini is darker and milder in flavour.

tamarind – a sour-tasting paste derived from the fruit of the tamarind tree.

tempeh – a traditional Indonesian fermented soy food made from whole soy beans, water and a special mould. High in protein and easily digested when sautéed.

tofu – coagulated soy milk curd processed with nigari, a sea salt derivative. High in protein and calcium (depending on its production). Can be purchased firm or silken.

umeboshi plum – a salted, pickled plum that is usually aged for several years. Its red colour is derived from the perilla leaves included in the pickling process. Use as a condiment and seasoning.

wakame – a delicate sea vegetable that is traditionally included in Japanese miso soup. It requires little soaking and has a mild flavour.

Index

215

218

Inspiring reading

For those who are interested in exploring the benefits of cooking with more depth, I recommend a few books that continue to inspire me to experiment and broaden my horizons.

Abehsera, M., **Zen Macrobiotic Cooking**, Citadel Press, 1971

Colbin, A., **Food and Healing**, Ballantine Books, 1986

Cook, W. E., **Foodwise**, Clairview Books, 2003

Erasmus, U., **Fats that Heal and Fats that Kill**, Alive Books, 1993

Gagne, S., **Energetics of Food**, Spiral Sciences, 1990

Organic and Wholefoods, Culinaria series, Konemann, 1997

Pitchford, P., **Healing with Wholefoods: Oriental Traditions and Modern Nutrition**, North Atlantic Books, 1993

Santa Maria, J., **Anna Yoga: The Yoga of Food**, Rider and Company, 1978

Sustainable Cuisine: White Papers, Earth Pledge Foundation, N.Y., 1999

With thanks …

This is my chance to offer my deep gratitude to those who have contributed to this book knowingly and unknowingly.

I'd like to bow to the team at Hardie Grant, with special and sincere thanks to Mary Small for her belief in me and for making this happen. A big thanks to the wonderful Ellie Smith for seeing it through and putting it all together – you really kept us on track.

A heartfelt thank you to Chris Chen for her graceful presence and awesome photos. Thank you to Trisha Garner and her design team for making it look so gorgeous. A hand-shake to Paul McNally, for his patience and careful editing. A big hug to Georgia Young for bringing along her entire china collection and a deep thank you to Debbie Kaloper for her exquisite styling and amazing friendship and support along the way.

My hands also go out to two pioneering men who have made wholefood ingredients easily available in Australia and who happily supplied me with ingredients. Thank you to Don Lazzaro, head of Pureharvest, and Jim Wilson, head of Spiral Foods.

To my wife Helen, thank you for your constant loving support, inspiration and wise words along the way. I also want to thank you for the changes you made to the recipes, and for tasting, editing and adding when I thought it would do.

To all those past and present who have encouraged me to write this book, I gladly offer you this creation.

To you all, I bow with gratitude and thanks.

Tony Chiodo

Published in 2010 by
Hardie Grant Books
85 High Street
Prahran, Victoria 3181, Australia
www.hardiegrant.com.au

Copyright text © 2010 Tony Chiodo
Copyright photography © 2010 Chris Chen

Cataloguing-in-Publication data is available from the
National Library of Australia.

ISBN 978 174270 491 3

Cover and text design by Trisha Garner
Typesetting by Pauline Haas
Photography by Chris Chen
Prop styling by Georgia Young
Food styling by Deborah Kaloper
Colour reproduction by Splitting Image Colour Studio
Printed and bound in China by C & C Offset Printing

10 9 8 7 6 5 4 3 2 1

The publisher would like to thank the following
for their generosity in supplying props for the book:
Market Import, Izzi & Popo, Made in Japan and
Womango.